Involved in the theatrical caper are:

BORIS KORSKY-RIMSAKOV: by his own admission the world's greatest opera singer, and an Official National Treasure of the French Republic.

DON RHOTTEN (pronounced Row-ten): America's favorite young TV newscaster, who is totally unrecognizable without his wig and teeth.

STEVEN J. HARRIS: probably the largest and ugliest state trooper alive, with a genius for delivering babies without benefit of a medical license.

ZELDA SPINOPOLOUS: a deliciously shaped biologist with no taste for the theater even though she has some spectacular talents—for example, she can revolve her left eye while keeping the right one stationary!

MASH GOES TO HOLLYWOOD
is an original POCKET BOOK edition.

Published by POCKET BOOKS

M✶A✶S✶H
Goes to Hollywood

Richard Hooker
and
William E. Butterworth

PUBLISHED BY POCKET BOOKS NEW YORK

M*A*S*H GOES TO HOLLYWOOD

POCKET BOOK edition published April, 1976

This original POCKET BOOK edition is printed from brand-new
plates made from newly set, clear, easy-to-read type.
POCKET BOOK editions are published by
POCKET BOOKS,
a division of Simon & Schuster, Inc.,
A GULF+WESTERN COMPANY
630 Fifth Avenue,
New York, N.Y. 10020.
Trademarks registered in the United States
and other countries.

In fond memory of
Malcolm Reiss,
gentleman literary agent

June 3, 1905–December 17, 1975

—Richard Hooker
and W. E. Butterworth

Chapter One

At three-fifteen one bright spring afternoon, Dr. Benjamin Franklin Pierce, fellow of the American College of Surgeons and chief of surgery of the Spruce Harbor, Maine, Medical Center was standing at the window of his office idly sipping a martini when he saw an official vehicle of the state of Maine pull off the highway and roll to a stop before the Emergency door.

The vehicle was a state police car. More precisely, a state police station wagon. It had STATE TROOPER painted on the doors and a large, chrome-plated device with flashing blue lights and a police whooper mounted on the roof. The lights were not flashing, and the whooper was not whooping, and the vehicle had been moving very slowly, as if the driver wanted to ensure a smooth ride.

Dr. Pierce removed the toothpick, on which two olives were neatly impaled, from his martini glass. He slid one of the two olives off onto his thumb and replaced the toothpick and remaining olive in the glass. He then flipped the olive resting on his thumb into the air, as a boy would shoot a marble. Then, skillfully balancing the martini glass so as not to lose a drop, he quickly maneuvered his head under the airborne olive as it, responding to the theorem that what goes up must come down, reached the apex of its trajectory and began to descend. His head tilted back; his mouth opened; the olive disappeared into his mouth; his mouth closed. He returned his attention to the Emergency entrance, sipping again at his martini.

The driver's door of the state trooper station wagon opened, and an officer of the law got out. He was a very large officer of the law. Dr. Pierce estimated that he must weigh about 230 pounds and that he was at least six-feet-four-inches tall. He was also, Dr. Pierce realized, facing the fact squarely, one of the ugliest human beings he had ever seen. He was built on the lines of a gorilla, including the arrangement of the nose, eyes, and mouth. When he put on his Smokey-the-Bear hat, it sat atop his massive skull like a fly on an ice-cream cone.

Dr. Pierce finished his martini as he watched the enormous, ugly trooper walk to the rear of the station wagon, open the door, and slide in. He then disposed of the second olive as he had the first, never taking his eyes from the station wagon except for a brief flicker of diversion to locate the airborne olive.

The trooper reemerged from the station wagon carrying a small, pink, blanket-wrapped bundle. He carried it with infinite tenderness, and a smile, incongruously tender, softened (if not much) what could only be described as his frightening countenance. Then (if this is possible), even more incongruously, he tiptoed toward the Emergency entrance, his lips forming what could only be the sound Mrs. Pierce had so often made to the fruit of the Pierce union: Coochy-coochy-coo!

Dr. Pierce turned from the window. He set the empty martini glass in the CONFIDENTIAL drawer of his filing cabinet, slid the drawer closed, walked to his desk, and dialed the number of the hospital telephone and paging system operator.

"Hazel," he said, "this is Hawkeye. Got any idea where Trapper John is?"

"Probably asleep in Intensive Care," Hazel replied. "Things have been slow up there."

"See if you can find him," Hawkeye ordered. "Have him meet me in Emergency right away."

"Got an emergency?"

"No," Dr. Benjamin Pierce replied. "We're gonna fool around with the nurses a little."

He hung up the telephone and started out of his office, pausing only long enough to pull up his necktie, slip into a white medical tunic, and liberally spray the interior of his mouth with a substance guaranteed to mask what its manufacturer euphemistically referred to as that "telltale party smell."

Dr. Pierce, having begun his professional day at shortly after six that morning with the excising of a kidney and having gone from that, with brief respites for coffee and doughnuts, through what are known as six other surgical procedures, had not intended to go forth among the patients and staff of Spruce Harbor Medical Center anymore that day. The breath killer was necessary not to hide the fact that he'd had a belt, with the implication that he was an afternoon drinker (which he readily admitted), but rather as a kind gesture toward those still on duty who would smell the booze and feel deprived and jealous.

As he marched down the corridor, the public address system, starting with a dulcet little chime, came into action.

"Dr. McIntyre," the voice purred. "Dr. McIntyre. Please report to Dr. Pierce in Emergency." Hawkeye winced. "Dr. McIntyre," the voice purred again. "Report to Dr. Pierce in Emergency."

Dr. McIntyre's full name was John Francis Xavier McIntyre, M.D., and he too was a fellow of the American College of Surgeons. He entered the left-hand door to the Emergency Room at a dead run, his hair somewhat mussed, his green surgical shirt buttoned incorrectly, and looking as if he had just been roused from a sound sleep. He had.

He spotted Dr. Pierce, who walked slowly into the Emergency Room from the right-hand door.

"What's the emergency?" Dr. McIntyre inquired.

"There is no emergency," Dr. Pierce replied. "You have leapt to a conclusion."

"You've been drinking," Dr. McIntyre accused.

"How dare you make such a shocking allegation?"

"I can smell the Booze-Be-Gone," Dr. McIntyre said, triumphantly. He looked around the room. "Where's the intern and the nurse?" he asked.

"In just a moment or two," he said, "the nurse will wheel in a lady who has recently become a mother."

"How do you know?"

Dr. Pierce raised his hand, like a traffic policeman, in the "stop" gesture.

"The infant, I daresay," he said, "is at this very moment being examined by Whatsisname, that splendid budding physician, the intern."

"What are we doing here? Is something wrong with the kid? Or the mother?"

"I would be very surprised if anything was," Dr. Pierce replied. "A complete examination, of course, is in order and will take place. But to judge from surface appearances, mother and child are doing very well."

"Hawkeye, what's going on?"

At that moment, the door sprung open from outside and a hospital cart was wheeled in by two student nurses as the registered nurse on duty hovered by. The cart held a dark-haired woman, wide-awake, who smiled softly.

"Congratulations, Madame DeBois," Dr. Pierce said.

"What was it this time, Antoinette?" Trapper asked.

" 'Nudder boy," the mother said.

"That makes seven?"

"Six. The last was a girl," she said.

"Pardon me," Dr. Pierce said. "Everything went well, I guess?"

"No trouble at all, except wit' Pierre," she said.

"What happened to Pierre?" Pierre was M. DeBois, her husband.

"He got drunk again," Antoinette said. "Every time, he do dat."

"Why not?" Dr. Pierce said. "And I gather that Dr. Smith just happened by at the right time?"

"Yeah," she said. "Dr. Smith."

"We'll put you in bed overnight, Antoinette," Dr.

Pierce said. "Just routine. I'm sure that if Dr. Smith had run into trouble, he'd have sent a little note or something. We're looking at the baby now, and when we make sure that he's all right, we'll have a little look at you."

"T'ank you, Hawkeye," Antoinette said. *"Comment ce va,* Trapper?"

"Just fine, Antoinette," Dr. John Francis Xavier McIntyre, F.A.C.S., said. Hawkeye nodded, and the cart was rolled further into the hospital. Then he led Trapper John into an examination room, where, after putting mouth masks on, the two of them watched the intern on duty perform an examination of the newborn infant. With two senior members of the medical staff, both of whom had a certain reputation for saying crude and impolite things in rather pungent language to junior members of the medical staff, the examination was lengthy, detailed, and careful.

Finally the intern looked up and smiled nervously.

"And what is your diagnosis, Doctor?" Hawkeye inquired. There followed a four-minute vocal dissertation concerning the infant's health and the factors on which the diagnosis was based. In layman's language, it was a healthy kid who had entered the world without difficulty.

"And your prognosis, Doctor?" Trapper inquired, when that dissertation had been completed. This dissertation required only about two minutes. The bottom line was that the kid faced no medical problems of any significance.

"We concur, Doctor," Trapper and Hawkeye said in unison.

"And if you could spare a little of your valuable time," Hawkeye said.

"Perhaps it would be a good idea to examine the mother," Trapper finished.

The three of them trooped into the hospital proper, marched down the corridor to Antoinette's room, and, with the assistance of the registered nurse on duty and with Hawkeye and Trapper John watching carefully, the intern performed a postparturition examination of the mother. The diagnosis and prognosis again were quite favorable. Mother and infant were reunited, and mother began to nurse baby boy.

"I'm delighted, of course," Hawkeye said, "but with Dr. Smith in attendance, not surprised. If he had run into a little problem along the way, I'm sure that he would have sent us a little note, giving us the benefit of his profound medical judgment."

"Like always," Trapper John said.

"Which brings us to the bureaucratic necessity of a signature for the birth certificate," Hawkeye said.

"Somewhat difficult to obtain from the attending physician," Trapper said, "since the good Dr. Smith is not here."

Hawkeye took Trapper John's arm and led him down the corridor. The enormous ugly state trooper was standing by the Emergency Room coffee maker.

"How's the baby?" he asked.

"Just fine," Hawkeye said.

"And the mother?"

"Just fine," Trapper said.

"We were about to hoist a wee cup to toast the baby's arrival," Hawkeye said. "Perhaps you would care to join us?"

"Thanks just the same, Doctor," the trooper said. His voice was very deep and had the timbre of a ten-penny nail being dragged across a slate blackboard. "But I'd better be getting along."

"I think," Hawkeye said, with a new and surprisingly firm tone in his voice, "that it would be a very good idea, officer, if you joined us. I have a message for Dr. Smith."

"Whatever you say," the trooper said, caving in immediately and somewhat nervously. Trapper John looked surprised. While Hawkeye Pierce was a tall healer, of good, even stocky, build, he looked positively wraithlike beside the state trooper. The trooper, in other words, was the one whom logic would dictate would be giving the orders and Hawkeye doing the jumping, rather than the other way around.

But the enormous, ugly trooper, holding his Smokey-the-Bear hat in his hands, docilely followed Hawkeye back down the corridor to his office. Trapper John followed. Hawkeye locked the office door and marched to the file cabinet.

"Dr. McIntyre will, I feel sure," he said, "have a martini. I will have a martini. I would be happy to make you a martini, Officer, a martini for which I am justly famous in medical circles. On the other hand, if you are not a martini fancier, I can offer you scotch, rye, and an incredibly potent potable known as Old White Stagg Blended Kentucky Bourbon, presented to me in case lots by a grateful patient. What's your pleasure?"

"Nothing, thank you, Doctor," the enormous, ugly state trooper said.

There followed a period of silence as Dr. Pierce concocted, with infinite care and precision, martini cocktails for himself and Dr. McIntyre. As he carefully added the precise amount of vermouth, he looked very much like an advertisement for a drug company, showing a dedicated pharmacist in the practice of his profession.

He handed a martini to Dr. McIntyre, who nodded his thanks, sipped it, nodded his approval, and then smiled. He said nothing. The truth of the matter was that he hadn't the foggiest idea what was going on between Hawkeye and the enormous, ugly state trooper. But Hawkeye and Trapper John had long been closely associated in the practice of medicine, starting with their assignment, long years before, as surgeons to the 4077th "Double Natural" Mobile Army Surgical Hospital (MASH) in Korea. He was willing, in other words, to indulge his pal in whatever he was up to, at least until he found out what was going on.

Dr. Pierce then opened the CONFIDENTIAL drawer of the filing cabinet and extracted a gallon bottle bearing the label OLD WHITE STAGG BLENDED KENTUCKY BOURBON.

The drawer was, in fact, filled with a half-dozen gallon bottles of the whiskey.

He poured a water glass half full of bourbon, looked at the enormous, ugly state trooper, and then filled the glass the rest of the way up. He handed it to him.

"I have the feeling you're going to need this," he said. "You may consider it a prescription medication, if you have mental reservations about saucing it up while in uniform."

The enormous, ugly trooper took the water glass, drank half of the contents down at a gulp, shrugged, and then downed the rest of it. Hawkeye obligingly refilled the glass.

"That's one of the nice things about being a doctor," Hawkeye said, thoughtfully. "You can prescribe booze."

"Indeed," Trapper John agreed.

"And there are other benefits," Hawkeye went on. "You get to wear one of these white coats, just like a barber."

"They come in two colors," Trapper observed. "White and green."

The enormous, ugly state trooper drank the second glass of Old White Stagg, this time without a pause, and Hawkeye filled it up again for him.

"Given a little time," Hawkeye said, "I could probably fill up the inside of a matchbook with a long list of the joys and special privileges of being a doctor."

The trooper looked at him uneasily.

"Not the least of which, of course, is the satisfaction that comes from placing into a mother's arms her new-born child."

The trooper's face turned white.

"In terms of satisfaction, that's almost as pleasant as knowing that your skill with a needle and catgut has saved a man's foot, after he has taken a mighty whack at it with a forester's ax," Hawkeye said.

The trooper, if anything, looked even more pale.

"But here we sit, chatting pleasantly," Hawkeye went on, "and we haven't even been formally introduced. I, of course, am Dr. Pierce. And this funny-looking fellow is Dr. McIntyre. And you, of course, are Trooper Steven J. Harris. Otherwise known as Dr. Smith. Isn't that so?"

The enormous, ugly state trooper set the whiskey glass down, exhaled, and looked at Hawkeye.

"In the army they called me Gargantua," he said.

"So I heard," Hawkeye replied.

"Are you going to press charges?" the trooper asked. It was a confession.

"I don't know," Hawkeye said. "The last time I encountered a make-believe medical doctor I cheered loudly as the cops hauled him away. This is a little different, isn't it?"

" 'Cause I'm a trooper?"

"No," Hawkeye said. "Because you obviously know what you're doing. What did you do, lose your license?"

"I never had a license," the trooper said.

"Who are you, the Great Impostor?" Trapper John asked. He had finally realized what was going on.

"I guess I am," the trooper said.

"And you didn't worry at all about the complications that sometimes occur in a delivery?" Hawkeye asked. "By what right did you risk that woman's life and her baby's life?"

"That was my one-hundred-nineteenth delivery," the trooper said. "I'd have radioed for an ambulance if I got in trouble."

"Your *one-hundred-nineteenth* delivery?" Hawkeye asked.

"Two here," the trooper said. "A hundred seventeen in Vietnam."

"Ah ha," Trapper John said. "You were a medic in the army."

"I was a Green Beret medic," the trooper said. "There's a difference."

"What's the difference?" Trapper asked.

"Green Beret medics get a crash course in medicine at Fort Sam Houston," Hawkeye answered for him.

15

"I should have thought of that. That explains the professional suturing."

"You better explain that to me," Trapper John said. "I missed something along the way."

"The army had a problem," Hawkeye said. "They needed a doctor to be part of what they call a Special Forces 'A' Team. There weren't that many doctors around, so they started training their own."

"You mean a whole medical program?"

"Sort of. In about fourteen months they taught guys enough to do practically everything a general practitioner can do," Hawkeye said.

"We were taught to do everything but open the cranial cavity," the trooper said.

"Appendectomies?" Trapper said.

"If we had to. Generally, it was surgical repair of wounds. But we also took care of the families of the Vietnamese soldiers. And that, of course, meant delivering babies."

"And you liked it, huh?" Trapper John said. He seemed torn between admiration and anger. "You liked being a doctor?"

"Yeah," the enormous, ugly state trooper said. "More than anything I'd ever done."

"And so," Hawkeye said, "you got out of the army and just decided to go into business for yourself?"

"No," he said. "I got out of the army to go to medical school."

"Then what are you doing in that state trooper suit?" Trapper John asked.

"I needed a job. I had to finish college, for one thing. And I'm not too smart. I knew that I could never make it through medical school if I had to work part-time. So I figured I could spend a couple of years as a state trooper, get my degree, and save some money."

"But why a state trooper?"

"It pays pretty good, with the overtime," the trooper said. "And I get an allowance for living in the woods."

"Plus what you make playing doctor?" Trapper John challenged.

"I never took a dime!" the trooper flared.

"No," Hawkeye said, "he hasn't. I checked that out last week."

"Sorry," Trapper John said. His frustration was evident. "But my God, you just can't open a clinic, free or otherwise. They'll throw you in the slammer!"

"How long before you can get into medical school?" Hawkeye asked.

"I'll get my bachelor's degree next month," the trooper said. "I haven't been accepted at medical school yet." He paused. "I don't think I can make it in this fall. But that's all right. That'll give me another year to try, and I'll be able to save more money in another year." Then he suddenly stopped. "That's what I was planning, I mean," he said. "Before I got caught."

Hawkeye looked at him for a long moment before he spoke.

"Caught? What do you mean, caught? As a member in good standing of the medical profession, I would, of course, make the appropriate outraged noises, if it ever came to my attention that someone was practicing medicine without a license. On the other hand, if Mrs. Antoinette DeBois tells me her kid was delivered at home, without medical attention, who am I to question her word?"

"You mean you're not going to turn me in?"

"Sure I am," Hawkeye said. "The next time you deliver a baby, I'm going to turn you in. The next time. Clear?"

"Thank you," the trooper said.

"You want to practice a little first aid, go ahead. You can also make some wild guesses about what ails people, so long as you don't pass out anything stronger than aspirin," Hawkeye said. "And as long as you make sure they come into town and see one of us. Understood?"

The trooper nodded.

"I think this concludes our little consultation," Hawkeye said. "Thank you for coming to see me."

"I really appreciate . . ."

"Before you get all wet-eyed," Hawkeye said, "don't get the idea that I'm doing you any favors. Wait till you get to be an intern. Making somebody an intern is a far nastier thing to do than sending him off to lay around all day in the slammer."

The enormous, ugly state trooper smiled hesitantly at Hawkeye and Trapper John and backed out of the office.

Chapter Two

"Wow!" Trapper John said, when the door had closed.

"Congratulations," Hawkeye said. "You've finally made it."

"Made what?"

"Become a felon," Hawkeye said. "You just failed in your citizen's duty to bring a lawbreaker before the bar of justice."

"I thought it was you that did that," Trapper said, moving to the martini pitcher and helping himself. "I was just what you might call an innocent bystander."

"We're in this together," Hawkeye said.

"In what together?"

Hawkeye took a form from his drawer. "This is the form that says we have investigated the circumstances of the birth, without medical attention, of that boy in the nursery and come to the conclusion that it was indeed a delivery at home, made necessary by the surprise arrival of the infant."

"That would be falsifying," said Trapper John as he reached for a pen, "an official document."

"Right," Hawkeye said. After Trapper John had signed the document, he signed it. They solemnly shook hands.

"Now what?"

"Now I think we should run up the hospital's phone bill," Hawkeye said. "Just to keep AT and T in business." He picked up the phone. "Hazel," he said, "I wish to speak to Colonel Jean-Pierre de la Chevaux, chairman of the board and chief executive officer of the Chevaux Petroleum Corporation, International."

"I'm sorry, sir," a strange, somewhat nasal female voice replied. "Hazel's off duty."

"Well, I'm sure you, whoever you are, will do splendidly," Hawkeye replied.

"The question, sir, is who are you? No long-distance calls are permitted from that extension without the permission of the hospital administrator."

"I see," Hawkeye said. "Hold on, please." He handed the phone to Trapper John. "It's for you," he said.

"Mr. Crumley heah," Trapper John said. "Do I infer there is some sort of administrative mix-up?"

"I just have your official memorandum here, Mr. Crumley," the operator said, "the one that says that under no circumstances are Dr. Pierce or Dr. McIntyre to make long-distance calls and charge them to the hospital."

"There must be some mistake," Trapper John said, rather skillfully mimicking the administrator's somewhat prissily effeminate tone of voice and manner of speaking. "That memorandum was dictated but not read. What I intended to say was that any calls made by those two distinguished surgeons and credits to the staff are to be charged to my personal account, as a small token of my esteem and respect. Now that that's straightened out, would you please complete the call?"

"Yes, sir. Of course. The calling party didn't tell me where I could find Mr. de la Chevaux."

"One moment please," Trapper said. He covered the microphone with his hand. "Horsey still in Alaska?"

"No," Hawkeye said. "I think he's with Boris and Hassan."

"I believe Mr. de la Chevaux can be located in the palace of the king of Hussid. That's somewhere in Arabia," Trapper John said.

"Arabia?" the operator asked, disbelievingly.

"Right," Trapper John said. "We'll wait." He hung the phone up and turned to Hawkeye. "You just want to say howdy and check in, or is there something else on your mind?"

"I think that the Chevaux Foundation* has just found a suitable applicant to lay some Jean-Pierre de la Chevaux medical scholarship money on," Hawkeye said.

"I didn't know there was a Chevaux Foundation medical scholarship program," Trapper John said.

"There isn't," Hawkeye replied. "But just as soon as I talk to Horsey, there will be."

"I don't think dough is going to be the problem," Trapper said.

"Dough is always the problem," Hawkeye said. "You have just heard my philosophic gem of wisdom for today."

"I mean it, Hawk," Trapper said.

"Explain yourself," Hawkeye said. "Speak slowly."

"Getting him into medical school is going to be the problem. Things have tightened up somewhat since they let us in."

"I have this sinking feeling in my belly that tells me that you may be right for once," Hawkeye said. "But no problem. We'll cross that bridge when we get to it. The first thing to do is get the money."

The telephone rang.

"Dr. Pierce," Hawkeye said, answering it.

"I have the Royal Palace on the line, Doctor," the operator said. There was excitement in her voice. The only palace with which she had previously conversed was Pasquale's Pizza Palace in Spruce Harbor.

"Congratulations," Hawkeye said.

"They say that there is no Mr. de la Chevaux in the palace."

---

* The Chevaux Foundation was established by the Chevaux Petroleum Corporation, International, at the suggestion of Colonel Jean-Pierre de la Chevaux (Louisiana National Guard), chairman of the board and chief executive officer. Operating with the income of 10 percent (1,089,344 shares; average market value, $44) of the shares of Chevaux Petroleum, the foundation has financed many good works, most notably the Gates of Heaven Hospital, New Orleans, Louisiana, and the Boris Alexandrovich Korsky-Rimsakov Memorial Home for Retired Opera Singers, Thespians, and Femmes de Pave, Paris, France.

"In that case, let me talk to the crown prince," Hawkeye said.

"The crown prince?" the operator asked.

"Right," Hawkeye said. He covered the microphone with his hand. "Horsey's not there," he said, "but since good ol' Crumley's paying for it. I figured we might as well say 'Howdy' to His Royal Highness."

"Good thinking," Trapper John said. "No sense wasting the call."

"Hawkeye?" a British-accented voice came on the line.

"Hassan, ol' buddy," Hawkeye said. "How they hanging?"

"I am in splendid health, thank you," the crown prince said. "And yourself?"

"Just fine, thank you," Hawkeye said. "Say hello to Trapper, Hassan." He handed the phone to Trapper and a few pleasantries were exchanged as well as the information that the weather was fine in Hussid, a little hot and dry, and the weather in Spruce Harbor was fine, too, although there was a hint of rain.

It was learned that Boris Alexandrovich Korsky-Rimsakov was expected in Hussid momentarily but regrettably was not available to talk on the phone. After four or five minutes of small talk between friends, at eighteen dollars a minute, Hawkeye finally got to the point.

"Hassan, we're looking for Horsey. Have you got any idea where he is?"

A look of utter surprise came onto Hawkeye's face at the reply.

"What's the matter?" Trapper John said.

"Good to talk to you, Hassan," Hawkeye said. "Say hello to Boris when he gets there, and take care of yourself. An apple a day, you know." He hung up and banged on the telephone switch with his finger. "This is Dr. Pierce," he said to the operator. "Would you get my home, please?" There was a pause. "Yes, operator, that was really Arabia and that really was a crown prince."

"What are you calling home for?" Trapper John asked.

"Mary?" Hawkeye said. "Is Horsey there?"

"Oh," Trapper John said.

"He stopped off en route from Alaska to Hussid," Hawkeye explained. "Hassan told me." Then he turned his attention to the phone. "Horsey? Hawkeye. Come on down to the office. I want some of your money." He nodded and hung up and turned to Trapper John. "I hope you're properly impressed that you were in on the very birth of the Chevaux Medical Scholarship Fund."

"I'll be more impressed if we can get Gargantua into medical school," Trapper said.

"If necessary, we'll have Horsey buy him one," Hawkeye said.

"I hope there's a good one on the market," Trapper said, "because I think that's what it's going to take."

"Certainly, Dr. McIntyre," Hawkeye said, "you're not suggesting that someone that you and I jointly, and together, with great enthusiasm, recommend for entrance into medical school isn't going to get in?"

"I'm not so sure I can recommend Gargantua with *great* enthusiasm," Trapper replied. "After all, all we've seen him do so far is obstretrics, surgery, and consultative psychiatry. For all we know, he may be a lousy internist."

"I think that's overshadowed by a certain natural ability," Hawkeye said, and his tone of voice wasn't mocking. "You really think we're going to have trouble getting him in, Trapper?"

"That's the way I see it," Trapper said. "There's only so many spaces, and twice as many . . . three times as many . . . applicants as spaces."

"In that case, we'll have to resort to blackmail, or whatever else it takes," Hawkeye said. "That guy's going to medical school, period."

"I think we can get him in, eventually," Trapper said. "But I don't think we can get him in next fall."

"We're going to try," Hawkeye said. He made another pitcher of martinis, and the two of them sat thoughtfully until the intercom in Hawkeye's office went off and announced the arrival of a visitor who identified himself as Horsey de la Chevaux.

"Send him in," Hawkeye called.

The man who appeared moments later in the office of the chief of surgery frankly bore little of the outward trappings one expects of a captain of industry. Instead of a banker-blue suit and a crisp white shirt, for example, he wore a woolen shirt and a pair of grease-stained work pants held up by fireman's suspenders. His feet were shod in engineer boots, and a knit cap with a tassel, the sort normally seen on small boys, rose atop his head.

"Goddamn!" he said by way of greeting. "How in hell are you guys?"

"Come in, Horsey," Hawkeye said, "and break out the checkbook."

Horsey came in, wrapped massive arms around each practitioner of the healing arts in turn, hoisted them off the floor, and kissed them on the cheeks. Then, without being invited, he went to the CONFIDENTIAL drawer of the filing cabinet and took out a gallon bottle of Old White Stagg Blended Kentucky Bourbon. With an ease and skill that could only be the result of long practice, he hooked his finger in the glass loop at the neck, swung the bottle around, and took a long pull from the neck. He then burped.

"You need some dough?" he asked.

"Right," Hawkeye said.

"For a good cause," Trapper said.

"How much?"

"About five grand for openers," Hawkeye said. "We'll be back later for more."

"You got it," Horsey said. He reached into the pocket of the grease-stained trousers and withdrew a folded-in-half stack of paper currency held together with a rubber band. It was fully an inch thick.

"Not even paperwork," he said, tossing it to Hawkeye. "Would you believe a king high flush?"

Hawkeye tossed it back.

"We need a check," he said.

"Cash is no good anymore?"

"We got to give a guy a scholarship," Trapper said.

"What kind of a guy?"

"A cop," Hawkeye said. "But don't get the wrong idea, Horsey."

The truth of the matter is that during his lifetime Horsey de la Chevaux had had many differences of opinion with officers of the law, generally centered around a differing opinion of what constitutes public drunkenness and disorderly conduct. Policemen were not among Horsey's favorite people.

"Give me the right idea," Horsey said. He did not throw the thick wad of bills back.

"About six months ago," Hawkeye began, "they sent a new trooper up into the woods. Soon afterward, we began to hear of a Dr. Smith."

"I don't understand you," Horsey said. He took another pull at the Old White Stagg.

"Well, normally when there was an accident among the loggers, the guy that got hurt came in here, damned near dead, wrapped in a bloody blanket. By the time they got here, in other words, it was often too late to save their foot, where they'd hit it with an ax, or run over it with a truck. And when their women had babies, because they didn't have any money and were too proud to go to the charity ward, they had them at home. That was generally a disaster, too."

"So who's this Dr. Smith?"

"Well, all of a sudden, when there was an accident, they came in here all neatly sewed up, or in casts. When we asked who had been the doctor, we were told that Dr. Smith, by coincidence, had just happened by and gone to work."

"So what's wrong with that?"

"There is no Dr. Smith," Trapper said. "The cop was trained by the army as a medic. He'd been doing all this. Including delivering babies."

"For free," Hawkeye said. "It took me a long time to catch on, because he'd really been doing a good job."

"So what's the problem?"

"For one thing, practicing medicine without being a doctor is a no-no," Trapper said.

"So I did some snooping around," Hawkeye said. "And Trapper and I just found out that the guy is working as a cop so that he can save money to go to medical school."

Horsey tossed the wad of bills back.

"My pleasure," he said. "If you guys think he'll make a good doctor, that's good enough for me."

"If it's O.K. with you, Horsey," Hawkeye said, "I'll pass this money through the Framingham Foundation. That way he won't know where it came from."

"Sure," Horsey said. "Let me know when you need some more."

"You're a good man, Horsey Chevaux," Trapper John said.

"Lissen," Horsey said. He was actually blushing furiously. "Anytime I can make a doctor out of a cop, I'm happy."

"So what are you doing in Spruce Harbor?"

"I was in Alaska," he said. "I got a couple of holes on the North Shore. Then Boris called up. Says he's going to Hussid, and if I ain't got anything better to do, I should come on over and play a little poker. So I remembered what Mary said about liking king crab, so I got some king crab and told the pilot to refuel here. You guys want to come to Hussid? It'll be like old times."*

"The offer is tempting," Trapper said.

---

* Colonel de la Chevaux and Boris Alexandrovich Korsky-Rimsakov, the opera singer, were comrades-in-arms during the Korean War. Both were hospitalized for treatment of wounds received in combat at the 4077th MASH, where Dr. Pierce and Dr. McIntyre were the attending physicians. The details of that relationship have been chronicled for posterity in a highly acclaimed, splendidly written book, M*A*S*H GOES TO NEW ORLEANS (Pocket Books, New York, 1975).

"But Trapper and I have a little work to do around here," Hawkeye said. "We are about to start a series of conferences with some of our professional brothers who have chosen to be associated with the teaching branch of the medical profession."

"It's only going to be for a couple of days," Horsey said. "I got to be in Caracas, Venezuela, on Friday. No trouble at all to drop you back here on the way."

"Thank you, Horsey, but no," Trapper said. "You said something about king crab?"

There came a loud, even imperious, knocking at the door.

"Go away!" Hawkeye called. "Can't you see the DO NOT DISTURB sign is illuminated?"

"Dr. Pierce," a somewhat nasal, rather effeminate voice said, "it is I, T. Alfred Crumley, the hospital administrator."

"Go away, T. Alfred Crumley," Trapper called. "Go wash a bedpan."

"And the chief of staff is with me!" T. Alfred Crumley added.

"You out there, Charley?" Hawkeye called.

"I'd like to see you, Benjamin," a dignified voice replied. There were few people in the world who dared to call Benjamin Franklin Pierce, M.D., F.A.C.S., "Benjamin." One of them was the chief of staff of the Spruce Harbor Medical Center, Charles W. Barclay, M.D.

"Just a minute," Trapper called. With what can only be described as amazing grace, the martini glasses, pitcher, ingredients, and gallon of Old White Stagg vanished into the CONFIDENTIAL drawer of the filing cabinet. An imposing array of medical documents, including three large X rays (specially prepared for just such an eventuality), were arranged around the room, mouths were sprayed with Booze-Be-Gone, and the door opened.

"We were in consultation," Dr. McIntyre said. "I hope this is important."

27

"I wouldn't be here if it weren't," T. Alfred Crumley said, sort of quivering in righteous indignation.

"You want I should wait outside, Hawk . . . Dr. Pierce?" Horsey asked.

"Not in your condition," Hawkeye said. "I wouldn't think of it."

"Benjamin," Dr. Charles W. Barclay said, "Mr. Crumley has come to me with a story that I find hard to believe."

"Is that so?"

"He reports that you have been placing international telephone calls and charging them to his personal number."

"He said that?" Hawkeye said.

"And I have all the details, Doctor!" Crumley said. "You're trapped this time."

"What details do you have?" Trapper asked, innocently.

"You just fifteen minutes ago placed a call to a Colonel Jean-Pierre de la Chevaux at the royal palace in Hussid."

"You're sure of your facts?"

"I'm sure of everything!" Crumley hissed. "I even found out where Hussid is! It's nine-thousand miles away, and the toll is eighteen dollars a minute!"

"Well, there you go," Trapper said.

"Dr. Barclay," Hawkeye said, "may I present Colonel Jean-Pierre de la Chevaux? Colonel Chevaux, Dr. Barclay."

"Mr. Crumley," Trapper said, gently, "as I'm sure you know, psychiatry has made giant steps in the treatment of hallucinatory conditions. Have you ever considered having a little chat with our own Dr. Wilson?"

"Obviously, Benjamin," Dr. Barclay said, "there has been a little misunderstanding. I deeply regret the intrusion."

"I just hope that we'll be able, all of us pulling together, to help Mr. Crumley," Hawkeye said.

"What would we ever do without him?" Trapper asked, piously.

"It's been a pleasure meeting you, Colonel," Dr. Barclay said.

"Likewise," Horsey replied. Trapper waited until the door had closed again.

"We were talking, I think, about king crab?" he said.

Chapter Three

Waldo Maldemer (pronounced in the French manner, Mahl-duh-mare) and Don Rhotten (pronounced in the Netherlandish, or Dutch, manner, Row-ten) were unquestionably among the most valuable assets of the Amalgamated Broadcasting System.

They were broadcast journalists who appeared each evening on the ABS Evening News for half an hour. As the result of contractual negotiations involving sixteen lawyers, two press agents, and Mr. Rhotten's mother, Hermione, in fact, the correct title of the program, as shown before and after each telecast, was "Waldo Maldemer and the Evening News with Don Rhotten."

Waldo Maldemer was a jowly gentleman in his late middle years, given to smoking a pipe and possessed of massive eyebrows that he could raise a full two inches to wordlessly express his displeasure with the news. Don Rhotten projected the image of a somewhat younger, more aggressive newsman, the image of nature buttressed with some mechanical assistance, including caps for his teeth, contact lenses featuring Paul Newman blue eyes, a large wardrobe of hairpieces, and a nyloncloth device with a lot of cords, which, when pulled tight, served to give his midsection the appearance of being a good deal less low-slung and bulgy than was the case.

Waldo Maldemer, in the quaint cant of the trade, "gave" the news and Don Rhotten the "comment." In both cases, what they read over the air with an aura of absolute confidence that was the envy of their competitors was prepared for them by a small army of anonymous *real* journalists, enticed away from honest employment on newspapers and wire services by the higher wages of what has come to be called the electronic media.

Freed, so to speak, from the mundane drudgery of searching out the news, the two were thus also free to devote their off-the-air time to such pursuits as addressing groups of potential sponsors of the program and advising presidents of the United States and other such bureaucrats on the conduct of national affairs.

All they had to do, in other words, to earn the $210,000 (Maldemer) and $185,000 (Rhotten) annual compensation paid them by a grateful Amalgamated Broadcasting System was to show up fifteen minutes before air time with a fresh shave and reasonably sober. To ensure that this in fact happened, both gentlemen were normally surrounded by a large staff who bore such titles as producer, executive producer, assistant executive producer, and senior executive producer and whose function it was to see that Waldo Maldemer had no more than three shots of Old MacIntosh Scotch Whiskey before he took his position before the cameras and that Don Rhotten's wig, caps, and contacts were in place. (There had once been a horrible blunder: Don Rhotten had forgotten his contacts. When his turn came to comment upon the news, all he saw on the TelePrompTer was a bunch of squiggly lines. Since he had, of course, no idea whatever what the subject of his comments was, much less the comments on his subject, there followed a full fifty seconds of dead air time, which is to television broadcasting quite as shaming as, say, a minister of the gospel getting caught whooping it up in a house of ill repute.

The staff had other functions, too, of course. Don Rhotten certainly couldn't be expected to either keep track of, or maintain, his supply of hairpieces, and there was an assistant executive producer for that function. Waldo Maldemer, confidante and golfing partner of presidents and chiefs of state, certainly could not be expected to answer his own telephone, and there was an assistant executive producer for that, too.

There were two large members of the staff whose function it was to protect the electronic journalists from the unwanted adulation of their fans. For reasons that only an experienced practitioner of abnormal psychiatry could possibly understand, both Waldo Maldemer and Don Rhotten were constantly under a sort of attack by a legion of fans whose sole aim in life it seemed to be to touch their heroes. Waldo Maldemer wasn't nearly as distressed by this phenomenon as Don Rhotten, possibly because Waldo did not have to avoid jerking movements of the head. When Don Rhotten moved his head too quickly, the wig would shift, either giving him an abnormally high forehead or moving the other way, blinding him.

At just about the time that Dr. Hawkeye Pierce and Dr. Trapper John McIntyre drove Col. Horsey de la Chevaux to Spruce Harbor International Airport where the colonel, full of Maine beer, Kentucky bourbon, and Alaskan king crab boarded a Chevaux Petroleum International 747, in other words, at just about the time that Waldo Maldemer and Don Rhotten were about to face the ABS television cameras, a strange apparition appeared in the corridor leading to the dressing room of Studio 17, ABS. (Studio 17 was a "permanent set" in the ABS Building. It was designed to look like a newsroom. There were genuine-looking, phony teletype printers, maps of the world, large numbers of unconnected telephones, and other such impedimenta. Plus, of course, desks for both Mr. Maldemer and Mr. Rhotten. Seven otherwise unemployable relatives of ABS executives were on the payroll. When Waldo and Don were on camera, they picked up telephones and mouthed imaginary conversations, looked at the teletype printers with rapt fascination, and so on. The newsroom itself, where the teletype printers actually printed and the telephones worked and where the army of formerly legitimate journalists prepared scripts for Messrs. Malde-mer and Rhotten, was in the second subbasement of the building. It was a dark, ugly room with battered furniture and could not, of course, be exposed to public view.)

It was a small human being, about five-feet-two-inches in height and weighing no more than 120 pounds, including a wristwatch with seven dials that must have weighed at least five pounds. This creature was wearing a dark blue jacket, sort of cut on the Mao Tse-tung–Nehru pattern, except that it had twelve large brass buttons arranged in double rows. The trousers were light yellow in color and close fitting. Since the legs were rather slight, the appearance was of a blue bottle suspended on toothpicks. There was an enormous amount of hair, sort of a spectacular Afro, except that the hair was blond and the wearer's face pasty-pale, negating any African connection. The most obvious conclusion to draw was that the gentleman had that very moment removed his finger from a light socket. There was also a very large set of round eyeglasses.

The creature marched down the corridor directly toward the powder-blue door with the large gold star and the words "DON RHOTTEN" painted on it. The junior assistant associate executive producers standing guard outside Mr. Rhotten's dressing room quite naturally believed that the creature was a fan who had somehow managed to evade the security guards elsewhere in the building and was now about to assault Mr. Rhotten with some outrageous request, such as for an autograph. Autographs were never given away. The selling of autographs was a nice little sideline of Don Rhotten Enterprises, Inc., nearly as profitable as the Don Rhotten Sweat Shirts and the Dandy Don Doll, which came in a box with six complete sets of costumes, plus a scale size model microphone and television camera.

The junior assistant executive producers stepped in front of the little man, barring his way.

"May I help you, sir?"

"I doubt it," the little man said. There was a harsh, unfriendly quality to his voice. Had the timbre of his voice been different—specifically, had it been deeper—it would have been menacing. But the timbre of his voice was not deep at all, and the result was that he sounded like a belligerent canary.

"This area is not open to the public," one of the junior assistant associate executive producers said.

"Sorry about that," the other one said.

"The public?" the little man squeaked. "The *public?* Do you have *no* idea whom you are addressing, you cretin?"

There was no reply. Canary-like or not, there was a tone of assurance, of self-confidence in the little man's tone that kept the junior assistant associate executive producers from picking him up and throwing him out.

"I am," the little man, drawing himself up to his full five feet and two inches, said, "Wesley St. James, *that's* who I am!"

The junior assistant associate executive producers paled. The larger of them turned and pulled open Don Rhotten's powder-blue, gold-star-adorned door. The smaller made a gurgling noise as he bowed. He was trying to frame a suitable apology and not quite making it.

Wesley St. James was Don Rhotten's closest friend, closer even than the Hon. Edwards L. Jackson (Farmer–Free Silver, Ark.), third-ranking member of the House Committee on Sewers, Subways, and Sidewalks. More importantly, Wesley St. James was in the industry, which is to say that he was also part of the thrilling world of television broadcasting.

Wesley St. James (it was pronounced Sin-jims) was in the entertainment end, as opposed to the news end, although it could of course be argued that Don Rhotten, on occasion, provided a lot of laughs himself and that, to tell the truth, most St. James Productions actually made strong men weep.

The words "A WESLEY ST. JAMES PRODUCTION" were, in the cant of the trade, "rolled on the drum" before and after such productions as "Life's Little Agonies," "The Globe Spinneth," "Guiding Torch," "One Life to Love," and "All These Children."

He was known in the trade as the "Napoleon of the Soaps," but that term didn't do him full credit. St. James' Games, a wholly owned subsidiary of St. James Productions, was responsible for the telecasting of such widely popular game programs as "Grovel for Gold," "Humiliation!", and the hottest thing on the current roster of shows, "Win Your Operation!", in which a panel of nonpartisan physicians, social workers, and clergymen decide which of three seriously ill participants would get an operation, absolutely free of charge, based (without regard to race, sex, religion, or national origin) on the participant's relating of the agony he was presently suffering.

The name of Wesley St. James was well known, but not St. James himself. His operation was based in Hollywood, California, and he rarely appeared on the East Coast and even more rarely in the ABS Building itself.

It was well known that Don Rhotten and Wesley St. James, two of the brightest stars in the ABS television heavens, were good friends and that they went back together a long way in broadcasting. Just how far back and where, however, was somewhat vague. Two very highly priced public relations experts spent much time and a good bit of money to obscure the facts.

The truth, known only to Mr. Rhotten, Mr. St. James, and Mr. Seymour G. Schwartz, senior executive producer of Don Rhotten Productions, Inc., was that all three of them went back to a 1,000-watt, two-camera television station in South Cedar Rapids, Iowa. Mr. Schwartz, who had entered broadcasting after the unfortunate failure of Sy Schwartz's Salon, a gentleman's hairdressing operation some years before its time, had then been known as Uncle Ralph. Every Saturday morning, Uncle Ralph and His Furry Friends, Big Bunny (P. Dudley Rhotten) and Little Bunny (Wesley St. James, then known as Wladislaw Synjowlski), had entertained the kiddies from nine to eleven thirty. Seymour wore a fright wig, straw hat, and overalls. Don and Wesley wore bunny suits. Seymour got a lot of laughs beating them over the head with plastic watermelons and baseball bats.

They moved upward, to a 10,000-watt, three-camera station in the university city of Rolf, sometimes known as the Oxford of Iowa, and it was there that Lady Luck touched them with her magic wand.

The anchorman (and only employee) of the Rolf station's news operation had dallied too long in the Elite Café. When he was finally located, he was rather, as Wesley St. James would say, "in his cups." Aside from the cameraman and the studio engineer, there was no one around to deliver the evening news but Seymour G. Schwartz (Uncle Ralph), Wladislaw Synjowlski (Little Bunny), and P. Dudley Rhotten (Big Bunny).

The show, as they say, must go on. It couldn't go on, however, with Seymour G. Schwartz, of course, because everybody knew him as Uncle Ralph, and all the kids would be expecting him to squirt Big and Little Bunny with a hose or wallop them with a dead fish, and no attention would be paid to the news. Wladislaw Synjowlski was out. The reason he was playing Little Bunny was because he sounded like a little bunny. Fate pointed its fickle finger at P. Dudley Rhotten.

P. Dudley Rhotten, au naturel, was not something to set feminine hearts aflutter. It didn't matter normally, of course, because you couldn't see him in his bunny suit. But he had to get out of the bunny suit to deliver the news. That left exposed a bald, rather bumpy head, shamefully naked except for a thin, bathtub-like ring of hair at the level of his ears. His teeth looked like a "before" photo in the *Journal of Corrective Dentistry*, and his eyes, sort of an off-yellow, were magnified by thick eyeglasses, giving him a somewhat guppylike appearance.

Seymour G. Schwartz, professional though he was, could not muster the courage to look at P. Dudley Rhotten on the monitor. He bowed his head and covered his eyes with his fingers, hoping that if Rhotten glanced his way, he would get the impression that Schwartz was at prayer.

An amazing, wholly unexpected thing happened. If you weren't looking at P. Dudley Rhotten, he *sounded* great. There was a certain quality to his voice, a timbre, an aura of utter sincerity that made him sound like a combination of Howard K. Smith, Dan Rather, and Walter Cronkite rolled into one. He gave the aural impression that the news had happened just as he had predicted it would, that he understood it and was passing his insights on to the viewers.

Seymour G. Schwartz listened to the news intently, something he seldom did, and found himself fascinated. It had to be the voice. Seymour G. Schwartz was well aware that P. Dudley Rhotten's total knowledge of history, world events, and politics could be written inside a book of matches with a grease pencil and that he had no idea what he was reading before the microphone or what it could possibly mean.

Seymour G. Schwartz did some serious thinking. With money borrowed from Wladislaw Synjowlski, obtained from a pawnbroker on his watch, and with the help of P. Dudley Rhotten's mother, Hermione, a company was formed bearing the new name, Don, that Seymour thought had more zing, zap, and powee than P. Dudley: Don Rhotten Productions, Inc.

The three, their fortunes now linked for fame or failure, set out for the big city and there encountered their first failures. Not only was there no recording studio in Council Bluffs, but the eye doctors and teeth cappers in that metropolis confessed that the cosmetic treatment of Mr. Rhotten was beyond them.

Undaunted, the trio rode the Greyhound bus into Chicago, where, in short order, Mr. Rhotten was equipped with a hairpiece to cover his somewhat knobby dome, caps for his teeth, and contact lenses for his eyes. He was then led into a studio wearing his new Sears,

Roebuck "Bouncy Boulevardier" suit, seated at a table, given a script, and filmed reading the news.

Wladislaw Synjowlski served as director and Mr. Schwartz as producer. Mr. Schwartz then rather skillfully spliced the film of Mr. Rhotten together with film of Messrs. Smith, Rather, and Cronkite as they read their news. After finding temporary employment for Wladislaw Synjowlski and Don Rhotten in the advertising business (they carried sandwich boards advertising Polish sausage up and down State Street), Mr. Schwartz boarded the bus for New York City.

For two weeks he failed to break down the barriers at any television network. Not only couldn't he get any responsible television executive to look at his film, he couldn't even get into the buildings. But if nothing else, Seymour G. Schwartz was tenacious, and he had both faith and imagination. It came to his attention that a very highly placed, very responsible Amalgamated Broadcasting System executive regularly sought a few hours relief from the press of his duties by going to the avantgarde cinema, specifically to the Bijoux Palace on 42nd Street, just west of Broadway.

With his last twenty dollars, Seymour G. Schwartz bribed the projectionist of the Bijoux Palace into slipping the Don Rhotten film into the program. What the rest of the audience, who had paid five dollars a head in the belief that they were to see a graphic, technicolor film of what transpires when two young ladies suffering from nymphomania meet two young men suffering from satyriasis in a motel room, thought when they got Howard K. Smith, Dan Rather, Walter Cronkite, and Don Rhotten instead has long been forgotten. What is remembered is that the ABS executive, placing duty above all, recognized talent when he saw it.

The rest is history. Don Rhotten was flown in from Chicago. He made his first telecast three days later. Within two weeks, ABS, which had traditionally run a poor fourth in the Neilsen and other ratings, had surged forward to capture third place and then second. A star, to coin a phrase, had been born.

Seymour G. Schwartz had only one remaining problem, how to get rid of Wladislaw Synjowlski. Big Bunny and Little Bunny, of course, has always been close, and their friendship had been strengthened as they marched up and down State Street in the icy winds carrying the Polish sausage sandwich boards, cursing Seymour G. Schwartz whenever they met.

This might, Seymour realized, give Wladislaw, or Little Bunny, the notion that he was entitled to a larger share of the action . . . which is to say, Don Rhotten Productions . . . than Schwartz thought was fair. Wladislaw would have to go

Wladislaw, however, recognizing a good thing himself when he saw it, didn't want to go. It took some time before Seymour G. Schwartz came up with a way to get rid of him. There was at the time a dramatic daytime series, rudely known as a soap opera, in rating trouble. The series, "Life's Little Agonies," had been a huge and long-standing success, but then the husband-and-wife team who owned, wrote, and produced it had happened upon the works of Dr. Norman Vincent Peale, and that distinguished theologian's works had turned around their lives and the series ratings.

They began to think positively. No harm was done, of course, when they gave up smoking and began to drink sassafras tea instead of 9–1 martinis. That was their business. But when the Power of Positive Thinking began to ooze into "Life's Little Agonies," that was something else again. There was simply no audience for a soap in which the heroine learned that she was not in the family way by her sister's husband; or where the missing $60,000 from the Widows and Orphans Fund, which Cousin Fred was suspected of embezzling, turned out to be a simple accountant's error.

Ratings dropped out of sight. The husband-and-wife team, when confronted with the situation at a high-level meeting, were unrepentant. Not only that, they were abandoning what they chose to call "Sodom on the Hudson" and television and were going to move to Bucks County, Pennsylvania, there to raise organic vegetables, breathe deeply, and practice positive thinking.

It wasn't a case of wishing them "Farewell, and good riddance." There remained six weeks of daytime drama to be written, filmed, and televised, which would capture a certain rating. Otherwise, ABS would be subject to payment of enormous damages to the various sponsors. The show had to go on.

But that, itself, proved a nearly insurmountable problem. No other soap producer would touch "Life's Little Agonies" with a ten-foot pole. They had their reputations to think of, and the taint of being associated with a happy, happy, uplifting soap opera would be with them all their lives.

It was Seymour G. Schwartz who came to everybody's rescue, including, he thought, his own.

He would buy out Wladislaw Synjowlski's interest in Don Rhotten Productions. Wladislaw Synjowlski would use the money to buy out the husband-and-wife team. No one but Little Bunny thought there was any chance at all that "Life's Little Agonies" could be saved, but that didn't matter. The way the new contract was written, Wladislaw Synjowlski, not the network, would be responsible for the payment of penalties in case the ratings the show got dropped below the established figure.

Everybody was happy. The husband-and-wife team loaded their goats into their station wagon and left New York for Bucks County. ABS executives wrote each other long memoranda congratulating themselves for getting out of a bad situation. Seymour G. Schwartz patted himself on the back for getting rid of Wladislaw Synjowlski with such skill and finesse.

Everyone underestimated Little Bunny. He did some thinking over one weekend, and by Monday morning he was ready to roll. He simply cut the old story off dead, where it had hung at the conclusion of the last episode. A new start was necessary, and Wladislaw Synjowlski gave it to them.

Instead of the traditional theme song, "Edelweiss," of "Life's Little Agonies" being played on the studio organ, there was a fifteen-second trumpet fanfare.

"Wesley St. James Presents," a dulcet-voiced announcer oozed, "Life's Little Agonies, Part II." There was then five seconds of silence, an enormous amount of time on a soap, and this was followed by a stomach-curdling moan of pain. The camera zoomed in on a hospital bed, on which a girl writhed in agony.

"Seventeen-year-old Martha-Jane," the announcer intoned, "pregnant by her Aunt Lola's alcoholic husband Anthony and seeking an abortion from friendly Dr. Grogan, whom she knows to be a secret homosexual, yesterday started out to have the illegal operation performed. Dr. Grogan's boyfriend, the Reverend Stephens, mistaking Martha-Jane's purpose in going to the Bonny Dell Motel and beside himself with jealousy, tried to run Martha-Jane off the highway in his car. He missed but caused a crash, in which Elizabeth Johnson, recently widowed mother of six, was seriously injured and may lose the use of the lower half of her body. Unnerved by the accident, Martha-Jane broke her solemn vow to Dr. Peterson, her Aunt Lola's secret lover, never to take drugs again. As she resumed her journey to the motel, she lost consciousness and wrecked the car. As this episode opens, Dr. Grogan, called from the Emergency Ward where the Reverend Stephens had just been admitted following his attempted suicide over losing Dr. Grogan to Martha-Jane, must make the decision whether to amputate one or both of Martha-Jane's legs. Listen now as Dr. Grogan approaches the helpless girl on the bed. . . ."

Martha-Jane groaned again, loudly, piteously, chillingly.

Wesley St. James was off and running. By the end of the season, "Life's Little Agonies" was back at the top of the ratings. And there were spinoffs: "The Globe Spinneth" traced the sad life of Aunt Lola's alcoholic husband Anthony, in his constantly unsuccessful search for sobriety. "Guiding Torch" touched people's hearts with the tribulations of a handsome, masculine man-of-the-cloth who was a little light on his feet. "One Life to Love" delved deeply into Dr. Peterson's dalliances with his patients, and "All These Children" asked the question if a one-legged young mother could find true happiness sharing her life and cold-water flat with the fathers of two of her three illegitimate children.

Under these circumstances, it was certainly understandable that Wesley St. James was a little miffed when he was not only not recognized by Don Rhotten's flunkies but mistaken for one of the common herd out there in television land.

Chapter Four

Wesley St. James, glowering ferociously at Don Rhotten's junior assistant associate executive producers, passed through the powder-blue door with the gold star and the words DON RHOTTEN and entered the sanctum sanctorum of television journalism's most beloved young sage.

Mr. Rhotten, wig, caps, and contacts in place and shepherded by Mr. Seymour G. Schwartz and two public relations experts, was in the process of granting an interview to a member of the printed media. This was, of course, a singular honor and privilege, and the printed media person was suitably impressed. Mr. Schwartz and the public relations men had had the foresight to buy the printed media person lunch before interview time and had succeeded in getting the gentleman quite plastered.

Just in case the printed media person's notes should be incomplete or a bit illegible, the public relations people had thoughtfully prepared a neatly typewritten transcript, perfectly suitable for use, in which Mr. Rhotten would come across as a thoughtful practitioner of his profession and dedicated to the highest principles of journalism, and the printed media person had asked questions he hadn't even thought of.

Some strange noises were heard. First a "Cheep, cheep, cheep" chirping sound, followed by a dull, flat crack, as if someone had stamped his feet on the floor. The printed media person shook his head to focus his eyes. He looked at Don Rhotten. A wide smile was now on his normally solemn face.

The "Cheep, cheep, cheep, slam, slam" sequence of sounds was repeated. Then, beaming with joy, Don Rhotten rose from behind his rosewood desk, where he had just discoursed at length on the problems France was having with its atomic power program.

He now had his elbows at his sides, his arms folded upward with the hands balled into fists under his chin. As the printed media person watched, Mr. Rhotten curled his upper lip up over his upper teeth, concealed his lower teeth with his lower lip, went "Cheep, cheep, cheep," and then jumped twice into the air, both feet at once, each time slamming them together onto the floor.

"Don-Baby, I've asked you. . . ."

"Shut up, Seymour," Don Rhotten snarled. "You've always been a spoilsport!"

From behind the printed media person, a strange apparition appeared. It was a small human being with a blond Afro and a blue Mao-Nehru jacket with gold buttons, and it, too, had its arms folded up, its fists balled under its chin. It bounded into the room in little jumps, both feet in the air at once, making "Cheep, cheep, cheep" noises from behind exposed teeth.

"Cheep, cheep, cheep," Don Rhotten went again. He bounced into the center of the room, his feet going slam, slam, slam on the thick carpet.

"Hi, there, Big Bunny!" the strange apparition in the blond Afro chirped.

"Hello, Little Bunny!" Don Rhotten replied, jumping up and down. "How's things in the briar patch?"

"Uncle Ralph," the little man said, jumping over to him and kissing him wetly on the forehead, "Little Bunny's glad to see you, too!"

Seymour, while he struggled to escape Little Bunny's affectionate embrace, gestured to the public relations men to get the printed media person out of the room. He shuddered at the thought of having it bandied about in the print media—as unimportant as that was—that Don

Rhotten had been seen bouncing around his dressing suite making like a bunny rabbit. Someone just might read it. My God, what Howard K. Smith could make of it, if he found out, in those snide broadcast-closing remarks of his!

Getting rid of the reporter was somewhat easier than getting rid of Little Bunny. Wesley St. James was perfectly willing to admit (in private, of course) that he owed his success, the private jet, the two Rolls-Royces, all of it, to Seymour G. Schwartz's wisdom and foresight. If Seymour hadn't set him up to take over "Life's Little Agonies," if Seymour hadn't shown his faith in him, why he still might be here as nothing more than a partner in Don Rhotten Productions, dragging down no more than a third of the $185,000 Rhotten got from ABS.

He was constantly showing his appreciation to Seymour. There had been gold watches, a sailboat, and, most valuable, at least six signed, full-color Bachrach photographs of Wesley St. James, all inscribed something like this: "FOR SEYMOUR G. SCHWARTZ, WHO MADE ME WHAT I AM TODAY, FROM HIS GRATEFUL PAL, LITTLE BUNNY."

Seymour G. Schwartz quite naturally loathed and despised Wesley St. James because of the presents. He was completely convinced that the gold watches, the sailboat, and the photographs had been St. James' exquisitely cruel means of getting back at him for having arranged for him and Don to parade up and down State Street in Chicago with the Polish sausage advertisements and a means to gloat over him. It was common knowledge in the television industry that Wesley St. James Productions (not to mention St. James' Games, which was a whole new ball of wax) made him the highest-paid producer in television. Wesley St. James had five producers who made more money than ABS paid Don Rhotten, and all Seymour had was a large piece of Don Rhotten.

With the reporter gone, there was no need for the wig, the caps, and the contacts, so off they came.

45

"Gee," Wesley St. James said, "it's just like old times, isn't it?"

"Not quite, Wesley," Seymour G. Schwartz said, oozing as much charm as he was able.

"Sure, it is," Wesley St. James said. "Just the three of us, Big Bunny, Little Bunny, and lovable Uncle Ralph alone against the world."

"But you're not really Little Bunny anymore, Wesley," Seymour G. Schwartz patiently explained. "You're Wesley St. James, the Napoleon of the so . . . daytime dramas."

"That's right," Wesley St. James admitted.

"And Dudley isn't Big Bunny anymore," Seymour went on. "He's *Don* now, Don Rhotten, America's most beloved young television sage."

"You're still Seymour G. Schwartz, though," Wesley St. James said. "Always looking for the black lining in every silver cloud."

"All I'm suggesting, Wesley," Seymour said, "is that it might be bad for Don's image if somebody saw the two of you doing the bunny bit."

"Don't knock that bunny bit," Wesley St. James snarled. "If it wasn't for Don and me, you wouldn't have made it as Uncle Ralph. You really looked weird in that wig and overalls, Seymour. More than one sweet little kid wet his pants in terror when you grabbed him."

"That only happened twice, Wesley," Seymour said, stung to the quick, "and you know it."

"Big Bunny and me were the stars of the show, Seymour. You were just the straight man," Little Bunny said. Don Rhotten nodded his agreement.

Seymour G. Schwartz knew that it was time to change the subject. Little Bunny had acquired a reputation, as Wesley St. James, as a man who should not be crossed.

"You're right, Little Bunny," he said, fixing a smile on his face. "So what brings you to Fun City?"

Little Bunny didn't reply for a moment. Then he smiled rather shyly. "I wanted to see you guys," he said. "I got a little lonely."

"Awww," Don Rhotten said, touched. "And we missed you, too, didn't we, Uncle Ralph?"

"We sure did," Seymour said. He looked nauseated.

"I brought you guys a little something," Little Bunny said. He reached inside his powder-blue Mao-Nehru jacket and came out with two small packages.

"For me?" Don Rhotten said. "Oh, you didn't have to do that, Little Bunny!"

"I know I didn't have to, dummy," Little Bunny said. "I wanted to." He handed one package to each of them.

"Wow!" Seymour G. Schwartz said. "A wristwatch. Just what I needed! This makes an even half dozen."

"They're engraved," Little Bunny said. "Don's says, 'From Little Bunny to Big Bunny.' And yours says, 'To Seymour, Who Made Me What I Am Today, Wesley St. James.'"

"How nice!" Seymour said.

At that point, Waldo Maldemer, one of the very few people who had access to Don Rhotten's dressing suite, came into the room.

There was an instant change in Wesley St. James. Gone was the gentle bunny.

"I didn't hear you knock, Hogjowls," he snarled.

"You remember Mr. Wesley St. James, don't you, Waldo?" Seymour said.

"Look at the watch he gave me, Waldo," Don Rhotten said. "You push the button and it lights up and tells you what time it is. You don't have to figure it out yourself."

"You ever consider a face-lift, Maldemer?" Wesley St. James said. "A little character, a few lines in the face, is one thing. But there's such a thing as overkill."

"I didn't know you were busy," Waldo Maldemer said.

"Since you're here," Wesley St. James said, "you might as well look at Seymour's watch. Show him the watch, Seymour."

Seymour reluctantly handed the watch to Waldo Maldemer.

"Very interesting," Waldo Maldemer said and smiled his famous fatherly smile.

"How would you like a watch like that?" Wesley St. James asked.

"I beg your pardon?"

"I like you, Waldo," Wesley St. James said. "I do things for people I like."

"Well, that's very kind of you," Waldo Maldemer said.

"And people I like generally do favors for me."

"What exactly did you have in mind?" Waldo Maldemer asked.

"You think you could hold your show down for a couple of days without Don?" Wesley St. James asked.

"What are you talking about?" Seymour G. Schwartz asked.

"Answer the question, lardbelly," Wesley St. James pursued, ignoring him.

"I think I could probably manage," Waldo said, somewhat huffily. "I was here before Don, you know."

"Yeah, and before Don you were so low in the ratings you'd have had to crawl up to get in the gutter," Wesley St. James replied.

"He's got a point there," Don Rhotten said. "You know that, Waldo."

"Don's not going anywhere with you, Wesley," Seymour said. He had finally figured out what Wesley St. James was leading up to.

"Shut up, Seymour," Don Rhotten said. "Nobody asked you."

"You and Don going someplace?" Waldo Maldemer asked.

"Here's the bottom line, Waldo," Wesley St. James said. "You cover for Don for three, four days . . . until Monday, and you get yourself a watch just like that."

"Where are you going?" Seymour said.

"You ever watch 'One Life to Love,' Waldo?" Wesley asked.

"Every day," Waldo said, firmly. "Could you tell me,

off the record, Mr. St. James, whether Dr. Peterson is really the father of Mrs. McGovern's unborn baby?"

"I wouldn't want to ruin it for you," Wesley said. "But do you remember what happened on Wednesday?"

"You mean when Mrs. McGovern came to Dr. Peterson and told him that she was going to have to explain to Mr. McGovern how come she was in the family way, after Dr. Peterson had personally sterilized him?"

"Right," Wesley said. "And what did Dr. Peterson say to her?"

"He said he would need time to think," Waldo Maldemer said. "When she told him she was in the family way, he stared into her eyes and said, 'Penelope, I need time to think.'"

"And then what?"

"Tears ran down Penelope's cheeks," Waldo said. "And mine, too."

"That's not what I mean, dummy," Wesley said. "What else did Dr. Peterson say?"

Waldo looked thoughtful and slightly confused. It was a well-known look. Millions of people had seen it. Waldo looked that way when someone in the production department screwed up and the big words on the Tele-PrompTer weren't broken down into little words.

"He said," Waldo went on, remembering the exact words and then quoting them, "'Penelope, I need time to think. There comes a time in every man's life when he must get away from the mad merry-go-round of life and go off alone by himself and think.' I thought that was beautifully put, Mr. St. James."

"I wrote that myself," Wesley said. "But you left out the important part, Waldo."

"I did?"

"'. . . and go off alone by himself *and commune with nature* and think,'" Wesley corrected him. "That '*commune with nature*' is the important part, Waldo."

"I can't imagine how I forgot that," Waldo said. "Probably because I was crying."

"Well, that's it," Wesley said. "It started me thinking.

I realized that *I* had to get off the mad merry-go-round of life myself and commune with nature, and do some thinking."

"I certainly can understand that," Waldo said.

"So that's why I want to borrow Don for a couple of days," Wesley said.

"So the two of you can commune with nature?" Seymour said. "That's ridiculous. I remember the time you two got lost in the experimental cornfield at the Cedar Rapids County Fair."

"Don't make me sorry I gave you that solid-gold-plated, five-hundred-dollar watch, Seymour," Wesley said.

"Where do you plan to go?" Waldo Maldemer asked.

"Deep in the Maine woods," Wesley St. James said.

"You're kidding!" Don Rhotten said.

"No, I'm not. It's all laid on. We got a guide and canoes, the whole bit."

"I get seasick in boats," Don Rhotten said. "Look, Wesley, why don't we go to Miami for a couple of days? Or Vegas?"

"What's in Miami? What's in Vegas? I'll tell you what's in Miami and Vegas: booze and broads. That's what's in Miami and Vegas."

"Right," Don Rhotten said. "We'll get us a penthouse at the Fontainebleau and have a ball! Seymour can arrange for the broads like always, right, Seymour?"

"Big Bunny, I thought you, of all people, would understand," Wesley St. James said. His eyes filled with tears.

"Little Bunny," Don Rhotten said, "if you want to go deep in the Maine woods, Big Bunny will go with you!"

"You mean that?" Little Bunny asked, choking off a sob.

"Sure, I mean it," Don Rhotten said. "Would Don Rhotten lie to you?"

Wesley St. James said nothing in reply.

"What's this, ho-ho-ho, Little Bunny—Big Bunny business?" Waldo Maldemer asked, ho-ho-ho-ing his famous ho-ho-ho.

"What are you doing, writing a book?" Wesley St. James snarled. "Mind your own business, hogjowls!"

"Sorry," Waldo Maldemer said.

"When are we going?" Don Rhotten said.

"Right now," Wesley St. James said.

"Right now?"

"I got a helicopter waiting on the roof," Wesley St. James said. "And we'd better get up there before the girls start wondering what happened to me."

"Girls?"

"Sure, girls. Big Bunny didn't think Little Bunny would go commune with nature in the deep Maine woods alone, did he?"

"Of course not," Don Rhotten said. "But if there's going to be girls, I'll have to wear my wig."

"So?"

"So when I wear my wig in the woods, it attracts flies. It's the glue, I think."

"So don't wear the wig," Wesley St. James said.

"How can I be Don Rhotten without a wig?"

"You got it. You won't be Don Rhotten. You'll be a simple nobody, Don. Think of that. What a change!"

"Wesley, you really are a genius," Don Rhotten said. "What shall I call myself?"

"John Smith," Wesley replied immediately. "John Smith. It has a nice ring to it." He pushed Don Rhotten toward the door and then turned to face Waldo Maldemer. "A word to the wise, hogjowls," he said. "My people will be taping your show. You try to stick a knife in my buddy's back when he's gone, you'll be back reporting on ship arrivals and hog prices before you know what hit you!"

"Trust me!" Waldo Maldemer said.

"Ha!" Wesley St. James said, and then he and Don Rhotten were gone.

"Can I see your watch again?" Waldo asked. Seymour G. Schwartz threw it at him. Waldo tried to catch it and missed. When it had bounced off the wall, Waldo bent and picked it up, put it to his ear, and then announced, "It's still ticking."

He was rather surprised when Seymour G. Schwartz snatched it from his hand, threw it on the floor, and jumped up and down on it. He stamped and jumped on it for a full minute and then, out of breath, picked it up and held it to his ear.

There was a muted buzz. The damned thing really was unbreakable. Seymour G. Schwartz began to weep.

Chapter Five

Across the wide Atlantic at just about this time, a moment that would live forever in the annals of opera was about to take place. The Paris Opéra, conveniently located on the Place de l'Opéra in Paris, France, was presenting Wagner's opera *Siegfried*.

Presenting this opus anywhere is always a major undertaking and generally a very expensive one. Often, presenting *Siegfried* costs the opera house a lot of money. There is an enormous cast and elaborate sets, and it has even been suggested that the opera itself is a little too long, a fact which discourages the sale of tickets to all but the most dedicated opera lovers.

This performance, however, had been sold out for three months, even though the tickets carried a one-hundred-percent surcharge as a "Performance Magnifique." A "Performance Magnifique" differed from a "Performance Ordinaire" in only one detail. That was the appearance of Boris Alexandrovich Korsky-Rimsakov, who was, by his own admission, the greatest living opera singer and possibly the greatest opera singer of all time.

This opinion was shared, fortunately, by many people and by the government of France itself, which had three years previously declared the singer to be an Official National Treasure of the French Republic.

It wasn't only that Boris Alexandrovich Korsky-Rimsakov was, in fact, possessed of a truly splendid set of pipes. He also had an unparalleled stage presence, possibly because he stood six-feet-four-inches tall and carried 250 pounds, with not an ounce of fat, on his frame. He habitually wore a thick, curling beard of dark black, matching his curly black locks. He had large, deep, piercing eyes.

For some reason, this combination aroused in the bosoms of women generally, and in those of French women specifically, a strange emotion. All it took was for him to appear on the stage and face the audience to cause a pregnant hush broken only by feminine sighs. When he opened his mouth and sang a bar or two, the sighs became moans of unrequited passion, and if he sang with his chest partially bared, women all over the audience gasped, groaned, moaned, and slipped glassy-eyed out of their seats onto the floor.

Whenever a "Performance Magnifique" was scheduled, it was necessary for the management of the opera house to erect what was known as the Korsky-Rimsakov shield. The purpose of the shield (a pipe and cyclone fence affair, rising from the footlights to the top of the proscenium arch) was twofold. First, it protected the cast and *Chèr* Boris Alexandrovich, as he was affectionately known, from a hail of hotel keys, perfumed notes, and intimate items of feminine apparel that invariably sailed stageward whenever the singer was on stage. (The shield was first used after the prompter was knocked unconscious by a rather substantial foundation garment tossed onto the stage by a Madame Marie-Antoinette Juvier, 55, wife of the deputy president of the Paris Bourse, or stock exchange.)

Secondly, the shield protected the singer from females who, literally beside themselves with passion, came racing down the aisle to leap onto the stage and throw themselves at *Chèr* Boris Alexandrovich's feet. The shield was, of course, impenetrable, but many a performance in which *Chèr* Boris appeared had to be interrupted while ushers and gendarmes pulled overwrought fans off the shield where they accumulated to the point that the other, merely glassy-eyed, female fans and the sprinkling of male spectators could no longer see the stage.

He was, of course, not only a great artist but a genius as well, and had to be treated as such. His little excursions from the straight and narrow path of righteousness were never condemned, at least by the feminine portion of the population. The complaints of the male population were dismissed, not without reason, as sour grapes. *Chèr* Boris Alexandrovich had only, as Madame le Président de la République told Monsieur le Président, only a couple of little faults.

These may be succinctly categorized as booze and broads.

The booze fell under the category of recreation. The broads were not, as he himself frequently pointed out, his fault. It was God's fault. God had made him so attractive to the opposite sex. It was his own private cross to bear.

He would have much preferred, as he often told his close friend and constant companion, His Royal Highness Prince Hassan ad Kayam, to have spent his life in the company of one devoted woman in a small house by the side of the road being a friend to man and lifting his voice in song only with the boys at the neighborhood bistro.

But that was not, so to speak, in the cards. God had obviously intended him to be what he was. Otherwise, he reasoned, God wouldn't have "seen him safely through shot and shell and near death in the Korean war."*

Instead of a small house by the side of the road, there was a fourteen-room duplex apartment on the Avenue de la Grande Armée, which *Chèr* Boris modestly referred to as his little *pied-à-terre*, or "foot on the ground."

---

* This is not one of what have come to be known as one of *Chèr* Boris Alexandrovich's "colorful little exaggerations." U.S. army records indicate that Pfc. Bob Alexander (his *nom de guerre*) served with distinction with the 223rd Infantry Regiment, 40th Division, as a Browning automatic rifleman, earning the Distinguished Service Cross and other medals for carrying a Sergeant J.-P. de la Chevaux off Heartbreak Ridge under a "murderous hail of fire, and while himself grievously wounded." The details of Maestro Korsky-Rimsakov's distinguished military service have been chronicled for posterity in the highly acclaimed volume M*A*S*H GOES TO PARIS (Pocket Books, New York, 1975).

This made reference to the fact that he did not confine his art to France and appeared, whenever the mood was upon him, at opera houses in Vienna and Salzburg, Austria; Berlin, Frankfurt, and Hamburg, Germany; all over Italy; and, less frequently, New York, Chicago, New Orleans, and San Francisco.

And instead of the company of one devoted woman, there were women in Paris, France; Vienna and Salzburg, Austria; Berlin, Frankfurt, and Hamburg, Germany; all over Italy; and New York, Chicago, New Orleans, and San Francisco.

The latter explained the friendship and constant presence of His Royal Highness Prince Hassan ad Kayam. His Highness had learned some years before that *Chèr* Boris' feminine discards were of far greater variety and much higher quality than those which came to an Arabian prince, even one with an income conservatively estimated at $30,000 per day.

Theirs was a mutually rewarding relationship. Hassan, to reiterate, got the discards, and *Chèr* Boris was relieved of the mundane drudgery of paying for things. The fleet of Royal Hussid Embassy limousines was at his disposal, as were the aircraft of Air Hussid, the Hussidian national airline. Hussid, whose petroleum reserves were second only to those of Saudi Arabia, provided thirty-eight percent of the petroleum needs of France. Air Hussid was thus the only airline in the world that could afford to operate the supersonic French transport *Le Discorde,* that graceful, droop-nosed aircraft whose operating costs ran to some $6,000 per hour.

His Highness, of course, was a devout teetotaler, which provided fine counterpoint to *Chèr* Boris, who generally began the day with an eye-opening four fingers of Old White Stagg Blended Kentucky Bourbon before proceeding to the breakfast champagne.

His Highness, moreover, had found in *Chèr* Boris and in his career a worthy vocation. Although he was heir apparent to the Royal Hussidian throne and Ambassador

Extraordinary and Plenipotentiary to both the French Republic and the United States, he really had little to do in France except endorse checks for deposit.

He had become, over the years, the de facto manager of the singer. His Highness was the man to see, for example, if you were the manager of La Scala and wished the singer to perform. And it was His Highness who took care of the little details that went with an appearance of *Chèr* Boris. He personally approved the cast, the orchestra and chorus director, and the stage settings and ensured that the Korsky-Rimsakov shield was in place and that the maestro's dressing room was equipped with a sauna bath, a well-stocked bar, a supply of the maestro's own recordings, flowers, and exercise partners.

Boris Alexandrovich Korsky-Rimsakov exercised regularly. He had three years before become a devotee of the physical-culture principles advanced by Dr. T. Mullins Yancey, whom he referred to as the Sainted Guru of Manhattan, Kansas.*

"I always sang magnificently," Boris had said, "but until I came to follow the tenets of that sainted man, never quite so superbly, with such feeling and insight."

Chèr Boris invariably exercised before a performance, and if the performance went well, as it usually did, afterward as well. His Highness kept the roster of volunteers. He and Boris both considered it a part of His Highness' responsibility to audition the volunteers. Art demanded it. An entire performance could be ruined if the preperformance exercise had been less than satisfactory, and as *Chèr* Boris so often said, "You can't tell a broad by its cover."

While variety was, as Boris put it, the spice of life, there were some performances where his exercise could not be a chancy, or hit-or-miss, proposition. When a role was going to place unusual strains on the maestro,

* For further reading: *Sexual Intercourse as Exercise* (498 pages, illustrated, $9.95) and *Health and Strength from Constant Coitus* (469 pages, annotated and illustrated, $9.50). Both by Theosophilus Mullins Yancey, M.D., Ph.D., D.D., D.V.M., Joyful Practice Publishing Company, Manhattan, Kansas.

nothing but the best would do. More than once, *Chèr* Boris had been forced to go on stage unnerved by unsuitable exercise partners. For reasons he could not quite comprehend, a number of volunteers, despite solemn promises to Hassan beforehand, could not restrain themselves from either talking during the exercise ("If there's one thing I can't stand, it's a chattering broad!" as Boris said) or, worse, professing undying love, passion, and gratitude.

All Boris required was the exercise. Anything in addition to the exercise distracted him.

Fortunately, over the years His Highness had been able to establish a second, far shorter, top secret roster of exercise partners who not only performed their duties well but fully understood and lived up to the obligations inherent in the privilege of being selected as an exercise partner.

The special roster for Paris listed but two names, Esmerelda Hoffenburg, the ballerina, and the Baroness d'Iberville. Both had unusual talents. The baroness, who had a Russian nanny as a child, had learned how to prepare blini (a sort of cold potato pancake served with sour cream and chopped onions), of which *Chèr* Boris was inordinately fond, and was, moreover, one of the few people anywhere in the world who could stay with Boris when he went at the booze. Esmerelda Hoffenburg's superb muscular control permitted exercise to take place when *Chèr* Boris normally would not be up to it . . . say, after he'd spent the night with the baroness, lots of blini, and a gallon or more of Old White Stagg Blended Kentucky Bourbon.

They were, moreover, fully cognizant of the great honor bestowed upon them. They had been called to serve again, something that rarely happened.

"Whatever else might be said about me," as Boris said, "let it never be said that I am selfish." What he meant by this was that it was really unfair of him not to spread himself around as thinly as possible. "Far better that two-thousand women should experience the thrill of their lifetime," he said, "than for one-thousand women to have seconds."

He deviated from this moral principle only when his art clearly demanded that he do so. It was only then that His Highness would get on the telephone to Esmerelda and the baroness to bring the tidings of great joy: "The maestro needs you," he would announce. "You may come to the apartment."

They invariably appeared within minutes, although there is nothing to the story that the baroness' Rolls-Royce always sat with its motor running waiting for the moment of glory. She merely had it waiting outside their apartment, twenty-four hours a day, seven days a week. The engine was turned off.

There was not, surprisingly, any jealousy between Esmerelda and the baroness. They had come to realize that there was, in fact, more than enough of *Chèr* Boris for the both of them and that they should spend the effort they had been spending upstaging, so to speak, each other making sure that no other names appeared on His Highness' special encore performance roster.

They had, in fact, been summoned to the Avenue de la Grande Armée apartment the day before. They had arrived bearing large wicker baskets of food and drink.

"I'm glad you're here," Hassan had said, as they came into the apartment.

"Is something wrong?"

"That American conductor, what's his name, Bernstone? . . . at rehearsal he muttered something about a *jambon** under his breath, and *Chèr* Boris, I'm afraid, lost his temper."

"Why should the mention of food annoy *Chèr* Boris?" the baroness asked.

"My dear baroness, I have no idea," His Highness said. "All I know is that *Chèr* Boris jumped off the stage, pushed Bernstone's head through the kettledrum, and then threw the kettledrum, with Bernstone still in it, onto the Place de l'Opéra."

---

* *jambon:* French for ham.

"And the performance is canceled?" Esmerelda Hoffenburg asked. "Is that what's wrong?"

"Oh, no." His Highness said. "The Ministry of Culture and Fine Arts sent a *Discorde* after Karajan. He was in Rio, but he agreed to come, of course."

"Of course," the baroness said. "But then what's the problem?"

"The maestro is melancholic," His Highness said. "I thought perhaps you could cheer him up."

"I think I know just what he needs," Esmerelda said, with a knowing smile.

"Darling," the baroness said, feminine menace in every syllable, "I'm first up this time, remember?"

"I'm sure," His Highness said, "that I may entrust our beloved maestro to your loving care."

"Of *course* you can, darling," the baroness said. "How long may we have him?"

"I'm going to the Opéra. The floor of the stage was dirty during rehearsal. *Chèr* Boris was annoyed."

"And well he should have been," the baroness said. She skipped toward the door to Boris' bedroom. "Boris, darling," she cooed, "it is I, the Baroness d'Iberville."

"The one thing I don't need right now is a sex-starved frog," Boris replied.

"I come bearing gifts, *Chèr* Boris!" the baroness cooed.

"What kind of gifts?" Boris asked, suspiciously.

"Blini and me, darling," she called.

"You may bring the blini," Boris said, "but keep your clothes on. I have enough weight on my shoulders as it is."

"If you're tired, *Chèr* Maestro," Esmerelda called, "I'm here."

"God!" Boris replied. "A frog and a hoofer! Is there no limit to what I must endure for my art?"

"Maestro," His Highness called, "I'm going to the Opéra to make sure the stage is clean."

"Tell the general manager that unless it is spotless, I'll mop the stage with him!" Boris replied.

"May I come in with the blini, darling?" the baroness asked.

"If it is clearly understood between you that there will be no bickering between you over who is to have the privilege of exercising with me," Boris said.

His Highness closed the door to the corridor as the ladies opened the door to the maestro's sleeping chamber. He rode down in the elevator and got into his limousine for the trip to the Opéra.

When he thought about it later, the whole horrible mess was his fault. If he hadn't really laid the law down to the general manager, there would not have been frantic scouring and washing of the stage and the props. That he could not foretell what would happen explained, but did not alleviate, the disaster.

At first, things seemed to have turned around and to be going well. Karajan arrived from Rio on the *Discorde* and immediately went to *Chèr* Boris' apartment to pay his respects. He too brought gifts, specifically a twenty-six-pound standing rib of beef, a small token of the respect and affection of the Rio de Janeiro Chapter of the Admirers of Boris Alexandrovich Korsky-Rimsakov. This was sent down the street to Maxim's for roasting and returned accompanied by a jeroboam of Château Rothschild '25 and the best wishes of the proprietor of Maxim's.

Boris' spirits rose. It was pleasant, if not surprising, to learn that Karajan agreed that Bernstone was tone deaf and not equipped to lead a Salvation Army street corner ensemble, much less the Paris Opéra, when Boris, himself, was going to sing. The twenty-six-pound standing rib provided a nice little snack. Boris was even willing to forgive the miserly proprietor of Maxim's for sending only one lousy little jeroboam, barely enough to wet his tonsils properly, and finally, both Esmerelda and the baroness remembered not to talk during, or even to offer effusive thanks after, the exercise.

Thirty minutes before the curtain was to rise, Boris arrived at the Opéra accompanied by His Highness, the baroness, and Esmerelda. The baroness herself volunteered to, and was permitted to, arrange his hair and comb his beard, and the general manager appeared in his dressing room to assure him that the stage and all props had been thoroughly scoured according to Prince Hassan's directions.

Boris left his dressing room for his triumphal entrance in good spirits. He even turned and addressed the girls.

"No promises now," he said. "But I may, between the acts, feel up to a little exercise. Settle who it might be between you."

It was, in a way, the calm before the storm.

The dramatic high points of the opera *Siegfried* revolve around swords. In the early part of the opera, Siegfried shatters one sword after another until he finally makes his own sword. The one he makes is so strong that when he whacks the anvil with it, the anvil shatters into little pieces.

All of this went well. In Act I, as Boris as Siegfried shattered one blade after another, his female admirers cooed and moaned. When he cut the anvil in half, there was a full two minutes of tumultuous applause, which Boris acknowledged by standing center stage, arms raised above his head like a politician.

He felt so good, in fact, that when he had finished exercising with the baroness, entr'acte, he told her that she could tell Esmerelda to hold herself in readiness for the intermission between Acts II and III.

Act II went well, especially toward the end, where Siegfried sings the plaintive line, "I am so lonely! Is there no one on earth to serve me as a comrade?"

By police count, thirty-seven ladies of various ages, shapes, and degrees rushed down the aisle to be his comrade and had to be peeled off the Korsky-Rimsakov shield.

In Act III, Siegfried heads for Brunhilde's rock to claim his bride. His way is barred by a character called the Wanderer, who stops him by brandishing his magic spear. Siegfried swings his sword at the spear, which shatters, and then proceeds to claim his Brunhilde. That was Wagner's intention, anyway.

What happened was that the prop master, driven to the edge of nervous exhaustion by the stage-and-prop washing, made a slight mistake. The spear he gave the Wanderer as he stepped onto the stage was a regular, ordinary spear of the nonbreakable variety. The sword that he placed in Boris/Siegfried's hand was of the shattering variety.

"Then I have found my father's ancient enemy," Boris sang, his voice rattling every last crystal in the opera's chandeliers and putting at least twenty-six matrons into a semicatatonic state.

Boris swung the sword against the Wanderer's spear. The sword shattered in his hand; Boris found himself holding nothing but the handle. He stared at it a moment in utter shock. There was no sound whatever, not even a cough, from the audience.

Realizing that the show must go on and that it wasn't going to go on until the spear was broken (which was the cue for the sound-effects and special-effects men to do their thing, causing thunder and lightning), he quickly improvised:

"I am Siegfried," he sang, rattling the chandeliers again. "Who needs a sword?"

He snatched the spear from the Wanderer's hands. Grasping it in his massive hands, he bent it double. It should have splintered, cracked, been rent asunder. Unfortunately, the spear shaft was not wood. It was of Miracle Lexlon, the latest American invention, guaranteed not to rust, fray, peel, crack, or break. When Boris released the pressure of his mighty hands and arms, the spear shaft snapped straight again, good as new.

"I'll be goddamned!" Boris said, momentarily forgetting himself. Then he remembered where he was and what he was supposed to be doing.

"I'll break your magic spear over my knee!" he sang, at the top of his lungs.

He raised his knee and brought the spear shaft down

on it. It bent double again and then immediately snapped straight.

He looked at it with disbelief and then raised his knee again. And again the spear shaft snapped right back.

And then it happened. No one knows who it was (the French maintain that it was a drunken American tourist, but there is no proof), but some man in the second balcony snickered and then giggled. The giggles were contagious. Within moments, from all over the theater, there was male laughter, loud, deep, belly-rocking laughter.

Boris Alexandrovich Korsky-Rimsakov was being laughed at!

What happened after that is not entirely clear. Three men were thrown from the second balcony into the audience, but it is not known whether the first man to laugh was among them or whether he was one of the four men in the second balcony who were dragged from their seats by outraged female fans of *Chèr* Boris and hung by their feet from the ornate, cast-iron gas lamps that decorate the outer facade of the Opéra building.

Usually reliable witnesses reported that just before the curtain was rung hurriedly down, *Chèr* Boris, apparently in the belief that Karajan was smiling, threw the spear at him. The spear missed the orchestra conductor but passed through the instrument of the second bass viol player, who thereupon went into hysterics.

There is evidence to suggest that most, but not all, of the damage to the stage setting was caused by Mr. Korsky-Rimsakov after the curtain fell. Some of the damage was done by his enraged fans, after they disassembled the Korsky-Rimsakov shield in order to obtain pieces of pipe foundation as weapons.

The last anyone actually saw *Chèr* Boris was when he went to Brunhilde's rock, more specifically *through* Brunhilde's rock, ripping it apart with his hands as he set out in pursuit of the prop master, with the announced intention of tearing the limbs from that functionary.

From that moment, he quite literally disappeared.

There was, of course, a good deal of confusion. The Honor Guard of the Garde Republicaine, who were, of course, standing in their full-dress uniforms on the steps of the grand staircase, were immediately summoned to quell the riot. Unfortunately, they were immediately recognized as males and set upon by outraged Korsky-Rimsakov fans. Only the timely arrival of the First and Second Phalanx of the Metropolitan Riot Squad, Gendarmerie Nationale (Paris Region), prevented the lynching of several members of the Garde Republicaine.

It was more than an hour before order was completely restored and someone realized that *Chèr* Boris had not recently been in evidence. He had not gone to his dressing room. Neither had he returned to his apartment. Nor had he made an appearance at any of his favorite bistros—Harry's New York Bar, the bar at the Ritz Hotel, or the Crazy Horse Saloon on Rue Pierre Charron.

It was, of course, naturally presumed that *Chèr* Boris was just a little upset by having been laughed at, and that he would, in a matter of hours, surface. An ad hoc committee of the Chamber of Deputies was quickly formed to present the official apologies of the French Republic whenever *Chèr* Boris reappeared.

When he didn't appear within eight hours, a discreet message was passed to the gendarmerie ordering them to locate the singer and report his whereabouts, directly to the office of the president, where the president and his wife would wait for the word.

When the gendarmerie were unable to locate the singer anywhere in Paris, the search was widened. But it was fruitless. *Chèr* Boris had vanished from the face of the earth.

Chapter Six

"And how did you find the martini, Dr. Pierce?" the white-jacketed sitting-room waiter of the Framingham Foundation inquired, hovering solicitously over the table.

"I just looked on this little table here," Hawkeye said, "and there it was. Now, please don't take this as a criticism, but it *was* a little wet."

"But I know the barman only put in six drops of very dry vermouth," the waiter replied.

"Well, there you are," Trapper John said. "That's twice as much as there should be."

"If you'll give me your glasses, gentlemen," the waiter said, "I'll take care of it."

Dr. Pierce and Dr. McIntyre, as if wired together, raised their glasses and drained them and then placed them on the silver serving tray.

"It wasn't necessary that you drink them," the waiter said. "I was going to replace them."

"Never let it be said that I'm a martini snob," Trapper John said.

"Waste not, want not," Hawkeye said.

"And just three drops the next time around, if you please," Trapper John said.

The waiter marched away, across the thick carpets of the sitting room, toward the sitting-room serving bar. It was a large, high-ceilinged room furnished with comfortable, leather-upholstered chairs and settees, the walls lined with books and large oil paintings of past Framingham Foundation presidents and distinguished fellows of the foundation.

Dr. Pierce was a fellow of the foundation. Dr. McIntyre was a special guest of the foundation. The rigid membership requirements of the foundation limited fellowship to those gentlemen who had been married for seven years, a requirement which Dr. McIntyre, despite his other obvious qualifications, did not meet. He was still a relative newlywed and as such could not be trusted not to confide in his wife certain facets of the Framingham Foundation.

Dr. McIntyre was allowed sitting-room privileges and use of the downstairs bar, the basement sauna, and the lower dining room. He was not permitted access to the upper-level dining room, the upstairs bar, the library, or the theater. Neither was he allowed to bring guests to the foundation's Cambridge, Massachusetts, home.

"I wish I'd gotten married earlier," Dr. McIntyre said, wistfully.

"I gather you refer to this evening's presentation in the theater?" Dr. Pierce replied.

Dr. McIntyre nodded. "And I can't go into the library, either, while I'm waiting for you."

"Well, I'm not going to leave you alone, Trapper," Hawkeye said. "I've already seen Miss Bonnie Bazoom and Her Dance of Desire."

"That's very good of you, Hawkeye," Trapper said. "I always feel like such a second-rate citizen when all the fellows go to watch the strippers."

"Terpsichorean ecdysiasts is the term," Hawkeye said, sternly. "I've told you about that before, Trapper."

"I'm sorry," Trapper said, humbly. "It keeps slipping out."

"Well, you're going to have to learn to control yourself," Hawkeye said. "This is the Framingham Foundation."

"It won't happen again," Trapper said.

"It had better not," Hawkeye said. "Ah, here comes the sauce!"

The waiter reappeared with two fresh martinis on his silver tray.

"I trust these will be satisfactory, gentlemen," he said. "Perhaps you would care to taste them?"

Both Dr. Pierce and Dr. McIntyre reached toward the tray, picked up a martini glass, drained it, and set it back on the tray.

Dr. McIntyre smacked his lips and cocked his head to one side. He nodded his approval. Dr. Pierce pursed his lips and closed his eyes. Then he too nodded his head.

"Very good, James," he said. "Bring us two more just like those."

"Now that you know how we like them," Trapper added.

"Very good, gentlemen," the waiter said.

They watched him march back across the thickly carpeted floor.

"Virtue is obviously its own reward," Hawkeye said.

"When the waiter comes back, I'll borrow his pencil and write that down," Trapper said. "A gem of wisdom like that should not be lost to humanity."

"Cast bread upon the waters," Hawkeye said.

"I suspect that you're leading up to something."

"I was simply thinking where we would be had it not occurred to us to petition the Framingham Foundation for a medical scholarship for State Trooper Harris, alias Dr. Smith."

"How right you are," Trapper John said, with feeling.

"At this very moment, Doctor, we would be in the gymnasium of the Mamie Luckenbill Junior High School, drinking lukewarm Kool-Aid and about to dine on baked beans and mostly meat hot dogs *en casserole*."

"I wouldn't want this to get around, Doctor, of course," Trapper John said, "but would it shock you to learn that I don't really care for the eighth grade school of art, even if the artist is one of your offspring and the teacher is my beloved bride?"

"Ah, here you are," Hawkeye said to the waiter. "How nice! I always think a martini is just the thing before dining on beef Wellington."

"Especially a beef Wellington preceded by oysters Bienville," Trapper John said. "Has it ever occurred to you, Doctor, how fortunate we are that our partners down life's long path are, shall we say, queer for mostly meat hot dogs and baked beans?"

"Gentlemen," the waiter said, "Mr. Framingham sends his apologies and asks me to tell you that he will join you just as soon as he solves a little problem with Miss Bazoom."

"Mr. Framingham is having trouble with Miss Bazoom?" Hawkeye asked, brightening.

"It wouldn't be a problem requiring the attention of duly licensed physicians and all-around healers, by any chance?" Trapper inquired, helpfully.

"I don't believe so, sir," the waiter said. "I believe the problem is logistic."

"I beg your pardon?"

"Miss Bazoom's pigeons were delivered earlier today, sir, the ones she uses in her dance?"

"And?"

"I fear the chef made a little error, sir. The pigeons were served with a nice little sauce *piquante* at luncheon. Rather well received, too, I might add."

"I see," Hawkeye said. "Well, I can see how something like that could happen."

"Miss Bazoom is rather distraught, sir. It appears the pigeons were trained."

"Trained?"

"Yes, sir. Apparently, when given the command, they picked portions of Miss Bazoom's costume in their beaks and flew away with it."

"Well, I can understand why she's annoyed," Trapper John said. "But I'm sure that Mr. Framingham can handle the situation."

"Indeed," Hawkeye said. "He is, after all, the great-grandson of our beloved founder."

"Quite so, sir," the waiter said. "Mr. Framingham asks the privilege of sending you a drink while you wait. Another martini, gentlemen?"

"That would make four," Hawkeye said. "I never drink four martinis at a sitting."

"So you'd better bring us two more," Trapper John said. "That will make a total of five."

"Which, of course, is perfectly all right."

The waiter made a little bow and left them.

Thirty minutes later, Mr. Matthew Q. Framingham VI appeared. Mr. Framingham was not only the great-grandson of the founder of the Framingham Foundation but also its executive secretary and general manager.

"Hello, there, Matthew my boy," Hawkeye greeted him cheerfully. "I trust the problem with Miss Bazoom has been satisfactorily resolved?"

"Resolved," Matthew said, sitting down and beckoning for the waiter. "Have you any idea how difficult one finds it to purchase trained pigeons?"

"I've never really given it much thought," Trapper John confessed.

"But you don't want to hear my problems," Matthew Q. Framingham VI said. "How, gentlemen, may I be of service?"

"We need to launder some money," Trapper said.

"What Dr. McIntyre means to say, Matthew," Hawkeye said, quickly, "is that we wish to pass some money through the foundation. The money will be used to provide a scholarship for a deserving young man. We wish the source of the funds to remain anonymous."

"A deserving young *man,* you say?" Framingham inquired. He was a very large young man, the sixth male of his name to be graduated from Harvard. He had, consequently, a rather odd, somewhat nasal manner of speech.

"That's right. We want to send him to medical school."

"I'm sure it can be arranged," Matthew said. "Just last week, Judge Kegley posed a rather similar problem to us. We arranged a full-scholarship, tuition, plus living expenses, for a protégée of his. A Miss Tootsie Mac-Namara. She will matriculate next week at the South Boston College of Cosmetology and Hairdressing."

"I know what you're thinking, Matthew," Trapper John said, "and you're about to get a knuckle sandwich."

"My dear doctor," Matthew said, "I have no idea what you're talking about."

"We have been thinking of Harvard Medical School," Hawkeye said.

"Which brings us to problem two," Trapper said.

"Which is?"

"Who do we know who can get him into Harvard Medical School?"

"That *does* pose a problem," Framingham said.

"You mean to tell me we don't have any Framingham Fellows on the faculty?"

"I believe that twenty percent of the faculty are privileged to be Framingham Fellows," Matthew said.

"Well, then, if a fellow can't do a fellow a favor, where are we?" Hawkeye said.

"You're acquainted with C. Calumet Hennesy, M.D., F.A.C.S., of course?"

"Is C. C. the man to see?"

"And Clancy C. Hennesy, his son, the distinguished radiologist?"

"Ol' Clancy owes me a couple of favors," Hawkeye said. "Are we then home free, Matthew?"

"Last week, Clancy Calumet Hennesy III, who last year graduated summa cum laude from Harvard College with honors in biochemistry, was informed that Harvard Medical School regretted there was no place for him."

"But his old man is professor of radiology!" Hawkeye said.

"And Grandpa, old C. C., is professor of chest-cutting emeritus!" Trapper said.

"As you can see, there are problems," Matthew said. "His name is Jasper T. Whaley."

71

"Who is he?"

"The director of admissions," Framingham said.

"And what's his problem?"

"He was denied fellowship, for the third time, in the Framingham Foundation."

"Why?"

"He's henpecked, and his old lady has both nutty ideas and a big mouth," Matthew said, lapsing momentarily from his customary manner of speech.

"She does?"

"Mrs. Eloise Whaley was reliably reported to have announced, at the Back Bay Petunia and Dahlia Society, that once her Jasper got into the Framingham Foundation, he would see to it that the doors were opened to the other sex."

"My God! No wonder he was blackballed!" Trapper replied.

"Heresy, that's what it is, heresy!" Hawkeye said.

"The membership committee vote the last time was eleven black, no white," Matthew reported.

"So he's retaliating by not letting anyone in who has a Framingham Foundation connection?"

"You could phrase it that way," Framingham replied.

"He's retaliating by not letting anyone in who has a Framingham Foundation connection," Trapper John dutifully phrased it that way. "So where does that leave us?"

"Gentlemen," Matthew said, "at the risk of disloyalty, of being asked for my resignation from the Harvard Club, there are, you know, other medical schools."

"Yes, we know," Trapper John said. "But we've already been turned down by the good ones."

"Harvard," Hawkeye said, "was sort of a substandard substitute. Under the circumstances, we were prepared to put up with it, ruinous as that was liable to be to his medical education, if that was the only way we could get Gargantua into medical school in the fall."

"Now what?" Trapper John said.

"Did you say Gargantua? What an odd name!" Matthew said. "Spanish, perhaps?"

"Now what?" Trapper John said, again. "Is anyone listening to me?"

"I think we better have another martini and think this over," Hawkeye said. "Although it seems right now if we can't get him in Harvard, we can't get him in anywhere next fall." He looked around for the waiter. He was nowhere in sight.

"Look at the bright side," Trapper John said. "A year from now, we can get him into our alma mater."

"One thing I can't stand is a professional optimist," Hawkeye said. "Where the hell is the master of the wet martinis?"

The waiter appeared at that moment, obviously distraught, and headed right for their table.

"Three more of the same, my good man," Hawkeye said.

"Excuse me, sir," the waiter said to Matthew Q. Framingham VI. "There is, I fear, a bit of a problem."

"You can say that again," Trapper John said.

"There is, I fear, a bit of a problem."

"Can't it wait?" Matthew Q. Framingham said. "I told Miss Bazoom I was having pigeons flown in from Brooklyn."

"It concerns a member, sir," the waiter said. "At least I think he's a member. He *says* he's a member."

"Get some black coffee into him and try to get him to bed," Dr. Pierce prescribed.

"The important thing is not to send him home in his present condition," Dr. McIntyre said. "His wife might get the right idea of what goes on around here."

"The gentleman is not trying to leave, sir," the waiter replied. "He's trying to get in."

"Well, then, what's the problem?"

"He doesn't have a key," the waiter said.

"You know the rules, Kegley," Matthew Q. Framingham VI said. "He signs the lost key card. You compare the signature with the card file. He pays the fine for having lost his key, and he is then given admission. We've been doing that for fifty years."

"The gentleman refuses to sign the lost key card, sir," the waiter said. "He says he's traveling incognito, and if he signs the card he will, ipso facto, become cognito."

"The rules are quite clear, Kegley," Matthew Q. Framingham VI said. "Paragraph 31, section C, paragraph al, I believe. Under those circumstances, the gentleman seeking entrance will be asked to leave. If he fails to leave, the assistant sergeant at arms will see that he does leave, forcibly if necessary."

"Who is the assistant sergeant at arms now, Matthew?" Hawkeye asked.

"Man Mountain Mulligan," Framingham replied. "Colonel de la Chevaux recommended him. There was some trouble with the American Football League. He apparently tore the arms off a rival football player, was suspended, and needed suitable employment."

"In that case, Kegley," Hawkeye said, "ask Assistant Sergeant at Arms Mulligan to be gentle with the gentleman. He may have his reasons for being incognito, and neither Dr. McIntyre nor myself really want to put the arms back on someone just now. Awfully messy, you know."

"Sir," Kegley said, "when I denied the gentleman entrance, he threatened to rip the bars from the door and come in anyway. At that point, I took the liberty of bringing Assistant Sergeant at Arms Mulligan into the matter."

"And Mulligan's really torn him up? Pulled his arms off?"

"Not quite, sir. The gentleman, at the moment, is holding Assistant Sergeant at Arms Mulligan upside down with his left hand while he's working on the bars with his right. It was at that point that I decided I had best bring the incident to Mr. Framingham's attention."

"Good thinking, Kegley," Framingham replied. "If you'll excuse me, gentlemen, I'll tend to this little problem."

Trapper John stood up.

"I can handle this by myself, Dr. McIntyre," Framing-ham said. "Thank you just the same."

"I wouldn't miss it for the world, Matthew," Trapper said. "I'm with you."

With Matthew Q. Framingham VI in the van and Keg-ley in the rear, the four of them marched out of the sitting room and across the wide lobby to the front door.

Everything was as Kegley had reported. Man Mountain Mulligan, all six-feet-two and 230 pounds of him, was suspended, upside down, by his ankles, which were held in the left hand of an even larger human being. The right hand of the even larger human being was twisting the wrought-iron bars protecting the foyer of the Framingham Foundation out of the way.

The bar-twister was neatly dressed. He wore a camel's hair, double-breasted overcoat and a pearl-gray fedora, one side of the brim curled upward, the other down. The fingers of the hand with which he was slowly, but inexorably, twisting the wrought-iron bars out of the way were beringed. The pinky held an eight-carat, square-cut diamond, and the index finger a ninety-four-carat emerald.

The face was somewhat unfamiliar, but the fedora with the sloping brim, the camel's hair overcoat, and the two rings were unmistakable. The ninety-four-carat emerald had once adorned the index finger of Sheikh Abdullah ben Abzug, absolute ruler of the sheikhdom of Abzug. The eight-carat diamond had once been the property of Colonel Jean-Pierre de la Chevaux. He had lost it in a small game of chance.

"Put the nice man down, Boris!" Hawkeye said.

"What happened to your beard, fatso?" Trapper John asked.

"You're not supposed to recognize me," Boris Alexandrovich Korsky-Rimsakov said, disappointment in every syllable, flipping Assistant Sergeant at Arms Mulligan around and setting him back on his feet. "I'm traveling incognito."

"It was the rings,* Boris," Hawkeye said.

"Of course," Boris said. "I could not, of course, under the circumstances, be expected to think of every lousy little detail. Now please tell that simpering simpleton with you to open the bloody door."

"He's talking about you, Matthew," Trapper John said, helpfully.

"Maestro," Matthew Q. Framingham VI said, "you should have identified yourself!"

"If I identified myself, you idiot, how could I be incognito?" He put his arms around Trapper John and Hawkeye. "Let's have a little drink," he said. "It's been a long and dusty ride from the airport."

---

* In addition to its intrinsic worth, the ninety-four-carat emerald, known to jewelers as the Star of Abzug, had a diplo-political significance. It had been presented to Mr. Korsky-Rimsakov by Sheikh Abdullah ben Abzug on the occasion of Mr. Korsky-Rimsakov's ennoblement. When the fortunes of fate threw the sheikh and Mr. Korsky-Rimsakov together for a two-week period (the details of which, for students of Arab-American relationships, may be found in M*A*S*H GOES TO MOROCCO (Pocket Books, New York, 1975) the sheikh had been so impressed with the singer's relationships with the gentle sex that he created him Sheikh El Noil Sniol (roughly, Lion Loins) of Abzug, Privy Counsel to the Throne. Subsequently, the singer was named Ambassador Plenipotentiary and Extraordinary, which position entitled him to a Royal Abzugian diplomatic passport, thus sparing him the boredom of having customs officials paw curiously through his luggage and granting him diplomatic immunity against prosecution for violating the laws of whatever country in which he found himself in the pursuit of his diplomatic duties.

Chapter Seven

"I have some good news for you," Boris Alexandrovich Korsky-Rimsakov, His Islamic Majesty's Ambassador Plenipotentiary and Extraordinary to the World, announced the moment they had taken seats in the sitting room and called for strong drink. "I will be spending some time with you. Incognito, of course."

"I'll bet that has something to do with your bare cheeks and chin," Trapper John replied.

"How perceptive you are, Doctor," Boris replied. "Where the hell is the booze? I wonder why I come here. The service is really lousy."

"Patience, Boris," Hawkeye said. "This may come as a shock to you, but many people regard membership in the Framingham Foundation as a great privilege."

"You're kidding . . ."

"Especially since the rules have been bent only twice to let in bachelors," Hawkeye went on.

"The other bachelor, I have been informed, is Framingham Number Six. Is that correct?"

"Correct."

"Well, his great-grandfather, or whatever, founded it," Boris said. "That explains special privilege for him. And odd that this should come up in idle conversation, I am, after all, the world's greatest opera singer."

"Why is it odd that it should come up in idle conversation?" Trapper John asked, innocently. "It seems to me that whenever you and I have a little chat, Boris, it somehow manages to slip into the conversation."

The waiter appeared. He set martinis before Drs. Pierce and McIntyre, and a busboy set up a wine cooler holding a jeroboam of Château Rothschild '36. The sommelier, with a nice little bit of showmanship, popped the cork and then stood waiting impatiently for the singer to sip the wine.

"It will do," Boris said, grandly. "Put another bottle on ice."

"You were saying that you were going to be spending some time with us?" Hawkeye said.

"Yes," Boris said. "I am."

"And to what do we owe this great honor?" Trapper asked.

"Something happened to me recently," Boris said, "the exact nature of which I'd rather not go into."

"I would love to go into it," Trapper John said. "You mean something actually bothered you?"

"Momentarily," Boris said. "But what it actually did was make me think."

"It really must have been something spectacular!" Hawkeye said.

"Stop interrupting me," Boris said. "As I was saying, it made me think."

"I don't believe it," Trapper John said.

"Here I am," Boris went on, "I thought. Going from one major triumph to another. Universally acclaimed, adored, beloved. And then I asked myself, what does it all mean?"

"I give up," Trapper said. "What does it all mean?"

"I mean, here I am, giving people all over the world thrills, beauty in their otherwise drab lives, and so on."

"So?"

"And then I asked myself the basic question, the bottom line. What's in it for me?"

"How about the women?" Hawkeye asked.

"And the money?" Trapper added.

"And fame?" Hawkeye said.

"Exactly," Boris said. "I finally realized that there must be more to life than women, money, and fame."

"How about satisfaction?"

"And satisfaction. I have that, of course, in my knowledge that I am the world's greatest singer. But the bottom line, again, is the answer to the question, is it enough?"

"I can't think of anything else," Trapper said.

"I really didn't expect that you would be able to," Boris said, and then he put his fingers in his mouth and blew. A mighty whistle resulted.

"What was that for?"

"I told you the service is lousy in here," Boris replied.

"You don't mean to tell me that you drank that whole jeroboam of champagne already?"

"I told you I was thirsty," Boris explained, patiently. He then raised his voice. "Bring the other bottle," he boomed. "And put one more on ice!"

"And what was the final result of this soul-searching of yours, Boris?" Hawkeye asked.

"Well, as I said," Boris went on. "There I was, on the stage of the Paris Opéra . . . more precisely, at the moment, behind Brunhilde's rock . . . when I realized that here I was, giving my all, enriching people's lives, bringing beauty and light into dark corners, that there were thousands of people out there taking all this in. And what, I asked myself, were they doing for me?"

"That brings us back to women, money, and fame," Trapper John said.

"That wasn't, I realized . . . it came as something of a revelation . . . I felt something like Brigham Young must have felt . . . quite enough."

"What else is there?" Hawkeye asked.

"I don't really know," Boris said. "But it occurred to me that if they were deprived, if only briefly, of my talent and genius, that they very likely could come up with something."

"And so you decided to visit us?" Trapper asked.

"Exactly," Boris said. "I thought it would be only fair of me to share, if only briefly, the drab, meaningless lives of people such as yourself."

"Gee, Boris, that's nice of you!" Hawkeye said. "I don't know what to say!"

"I don't suppose you considered visiting Prince Hassan's homeland?" Trapper asked.

"Or Hot Lips in New Orleans?" Hawkeye asked.

"Or Frenchie de la Chevaux?" Trapper asked.

"Or anybody else?" they said, in unison.

"Of course, I did," Boris said. "But they, like everyone else in the world, make such a fuss over me. I understand their awe, of course, but . . . and I would rather you didn't tell them this . . . it really is such a bore."

"Don't faint, Boris," Trapper said, "but you don't awe me."

"I know I don't, dear fellow," Boris said. "And that's why I'm here with you and Hawkeye. With you two I can be my simple, modest, self-effacing self."

"I see," Hawkeye said. "And how long do you plan to stay?"

"Not long," Boris said. "No more than three months. It really wouldn't be decent of me to deprive the world of my talent for longer than that."

"It's going to be a little bit of a problem," Hawkeye said. "At least at my house. My mother- and father-in-law are visiting us."

"Mine, too," Trapper John said. "And mine brought with them three uncles, two cousins, and a maiden aunt."

"That should pose no problem," Boris said, thoughtfully. "Under the circumstances they will certainly be willing to live in a motel."

"After all, it's not every day that Boris Alexandrovich Korsky-Rimsakov drops by for three months, is it?" Trapper John said.

"Precisely," Boris replied.

"May I make a suggestion, Boris?" Hawkeye asked.

"If you feel you have to," Boris replied. "My mind is made up."

"I think your idea is good, even brilliant," Hawkeye said.

"Naturally," Boris said. "I told you it was my idea."

"But I don't think you've carried it far enough."

"You don't say?"

"Yes, he does," Trapper said. He had no idea where Hawkeye was leading, but he knew his only hope lay in going with him.

"What, exactly, is it you're trying to say?" Boris said.

"Well, Boris," Hawkeye said, "Trapper's wife and my wife know who you are. Even without the beard, they'll know you."

"So?"

"And they'll be fawning over you,* just like the others."

"Well, you'll just have to speak to them and tell them to control themselves," Boris said. "We are, after all, dealing with my artistic life, and with that in mind, everybody should be prepared to make whatever sacrifices are indicated."

"What you need," Hawkeye said, plunging ahead, "is to spend your time with someone who has no idea who you are."

"Don't be absurd," Boris said. "Everyone knows who I am. My God, Hawkeye, try to remember that you're talking with Boris Alexandrovich Korsky-Rimsakov!"

"What would you say if I told you I knew of someone who had never heard of you?"

"If you think I intend to spend the next three months of my already too brief life in the company of some illiterate moron, Hawkeye!"

"Let me put it this way, Boris," Hawkeye said. "Trapper John and I have recently met a fine chap named Steven Harris."

"Splendid fellow," Trapper chimed in. "Nearly as big as you are."

---

* This was not exactly the truth, the whole truth, and nothing but the truth. The truth was that neither Mrs. Pierce nor Mrs. McIntyre was exactly a fan of *Chèr* Boris. The last time Mrs. Pierce had spoken of him, she had described him as "that drunken ape," and Mrs. McIntyre had described his singing as sounding like the sound made by a bull who had not quite succeeded in jumping over a barbed wire fence and was, in a sense, bemoaning his just-lost malehood.

"And he's never heard of me? What is he, some kind of a hermit?"

"Almost," Hawkeye said. "He lives in the deep woods."

"And what does he do in the deep woods?"

"He's a cop," Trapper said.

"A cop? You mean, a *policeman?*" . .

"More like Renfrew of the Royal Mounted, actually," Trapper said. "He's a Maine state trooper, who brings the law to the people in the deep woods."

"Go on," Boris said. "For some reason, this interests me."

"Far from television, of course," Trapper said. "He lives in a log cabin on the shores of a remote lake."

"How fascinating," Boris said. "He probably has to cool his champagne in a mountain stream."

"There would be one other advantage, Boris," Trapper said. "You know full well that your fans, not to mention Hassan, Esmerelda, and the baroness, will soon be in pursuit of you, if they're not already knocking at the door downstairs."

Boris looked somewhat nervously toward the door.

"You're right, of course," he said. "They'll pursue me to the ends of the world."

"The one place they wouldn't look for you, Boris," Hawkeye said, "would be in a log cabin on the shores of a small lake in the deep Maine woods."

"By God, you're right," Boris said. "But how would you explain me to him?"

"Can you still cook, Boris?"

"What an absurd question," Boris said. "Of course, I can still cook.* You know very well that I enrich the

---

* Mr. Korsky-Rimsakov's culinary expertise dates back to his experience as a short-order cook in the Dandy-DeLite Diner in Hackensack, New Jersey, in his youth. In the army, he had served as a cook until Sgt. J.-P. de la Chevaux had made him a Browning automatic rifleman because of his size. In his long years in France, he had returned to cooking as a hobby and had, in 1970, been admitted to the Grand Compagnie des Gourmets after revealing the secret (overnight marination in a bathtub of Old White Stagg Blended Kentucky Bourbon) of his famous delicacy, Standing Rib of Beef Korsky-Rimsakov, to the Grand Council of Chefs Française.

lives of my fellow humans in many ways in addition to my superb voice."

"Picture this," Trapper said. "You rise at dawn and walk to the water's edge, casting your line into the azure-blue depths. Then you take the freshly caught trout and prepare them for breakfast, on a wood stove, for which you had the previous evening chopped the wood."

"*Almondine,* of course," Boris said. "Or perhaps, in *beurre noir.*" His imagination had been fired. "With a side order of *pommes de terre Alsatienne.*"

"Right," Hawkeye said.

"By God, Renfrew of the Royal Mounted will know he's had a meal," Boris said.

"And think of all the time you'll have to think," Hawkeye said.

"Where no one would possibly think to look for you."

"When can I leave?" Boris asked.

"I'll have to make a couple of telephone calls," Hawkeye said. "To see if he'll have you."

"What do you mean, 'if he'll have me'? Who would refuse . . . I see what you mean, Hawkeye," Boris said.

"I'll do my best," Hawkeye said. "I'll ask him to take you on as his cook as a personal favor to me."

"You might mention the penalties for unlicensed surgery," Trapper offered.

"That thought had crossed my mind," Hawkeye said. "I'll go call. You stay here and get Boris something to drink." He paused. "Something stronger than bubbly, I suggest, is indicated."

"Gotcha," Trapper said.

"First the good news, Steve," Hawkeye said, when he got State Trooper Steven Harris, "and then a double dose of bad news."

"What do you mean?"

"I have just learned that the Framingham Foundation is going to award you a scholarship to medical school."

There was no reply.

"I don't hear you jumping up and down in joy," Hawkeye finally said.

"I don't mean to sound ungrateful or anything, Dr. Pierce," Harris replied, "but I promised myself that I'd pay for the whole thing myself. That way, if I flunk out, I won't be a disappointment to anybody."

"I see," Hawkeye said. "Well, that was the bad news."

"I thought you were going to give me the good news first."

"The first thing you're going to have to learn if you're going to be a successful doctor, Steven," Hawkeye said, firmly, "is never to argue with an older doctor. We're always right."

"Sorry," Steve said, chastened.

"The good news is that I have come up with a way for you to earn a little money."

"Great!" Steven replied. "Presuming it's honest."

"How good are you at handling crazy drunks?" Hawkeye asked.

"You have to ask? You know how long I've been working in the woods with the loggers."

"That's why I recommended you for this job."

"What job?"

"Tragic case," Hawkeye said. "Looks almost normal, but a real looney, especially when he's drinking."

"What do I have to do?"

"Well, he belongs on a funny farm," Hawkeye said, "but he's always so sad when they lock him up that the family has asked me if there wasn't another solution. Fortunately, they're loaded."

"What's wrong with him?"

"He thinks he's the world's greatest opera singer and cook," Hawkeye said.

"Real schizophrenic, huh?"

"Plus dementia praecox," Hawkeye said. "He poses no problem unless he suspects that people don't believe he's the world's greatest opera singer and cook, in which case he goes wild."

"I could humor him," Harris said, thoughtfully.

"He can, oddly enough, cook pretty good."

"Gee, that would be nice. I'm a lousy cook and so sick of canned food I could scream."

"If you can keep him sober," Hawkeye qualified.

"If it's a question of him doing my cooking or boozing it up, I'll keep him as sober as a judge."

"If that's the best you can do, it'll have to do," Hawkeye said. "I was thinking of flying him up there today. Could you handle it?"

"Sure," Harris said. "Is he drinking now?"

"Uh-huh," Hawkeye said.

"I can handle it," Harris said. "How long will he be here?"

"Couple of weeks, anyway. The family will pay you one-hundred-twenty-five dollars a day."

"You're kidding."

"If that isn't enough, I'm empowered to go to two-hundred dollars," Hawkeye said.

"I don't want to take advantage of anyone like that."

"My final offer is two-hundred-and-fifty dollars," Hawkeye said. In his mind he did the arithmetic. He had $5,000 of Horsey's money. At $250 a day, that came out to twenty days. That would give Steve the $5,000, and in twenty days, he was sure, Boris would no longer be able to punish the world by withholding his talents from it.

"I accept," Harris said, quickly.

"Good. I'll have him up there this afternoon. And if you run into something you can't handle by calm reason, compassion, or brute strength, Steve, you just get on the phone."

"I can handle it," Steve said.

"I'm sure you can," Hawkeye said. "I'll be in touch, Steve."

Hawkeye banged the phone until he had attracted the operator's attention again. "Operator," he said. "Person-to-person to the Right Honorable Wrong Way Napolitano, at Spruce Harbor International Airport."

Mr. Napolitano, who was sometimes known as the Lindbergh of Maine, was proprietor of the Spruce Harbor Flying Service, whose fleet of aircraft consisted of a J-4 Piper Cub and a DeHavilland Beaver mounted on floats. Normally, he was beside himself with joy when someone sought his professional services, but when he came on the phone today, he was reluctant to make himself available.

"I already got a charter flight, Hawkeye," he said.

"I need you, Wrong Way," Hawkeye replied. "Make the others wait."

"Gee, Hawkeye," Wrong Way said, "I'd like to help you out . . ."

"Good," Hawkeye said. "Leave for Boston Harbor right away with the Beaver seaplane."

"I got a charter," Wrong Way repeated.

"So you said," Hawkeye replied.

"Couple of nuts from the city," he said. "You know my brother Angelo, the lawyer?"

"Yeah?"

"Well, things have been a little slow in the law racket, and he needs the money."

"What money?"

"He's gonna put on boots and a mackinaw and one of them funny furry hats and be a deep woods guide. He's getting a hundred dollars a day."

"Wrong Way, Angelo can't make it from the jail to the police court without a guide. How's he going to guide somebody around the deep woods?"

"He don't have to. I just drop them off at the lake and pick them up five days later. If Angelo remembers not to get out of sight of the lake, everything'll be just fine."

"You can just carry my passenger with yours, Wrong Way," Hawkeye said. "All you have to do is drop him off at Lake Kelly, where Trooper Harris has his log cabin."

"I just can't do it, Hawkeye," Wrong Way said.

"I know it wouldn't do any good to appeal to your warm humanity, Wrong Way," Hawkeye said, "or to your well-known compassion for people in trouble. So I'll put it this way. Unless I see that beat-up airplane of yours descending to Boston Harbor in two hours, Madame Napolitano, your better half, gets to see the pictures of you and Angelo the police took coming out of the Dew Drop Inn, Motel, and Cat House. The ones with the ladies all wrapped, in the name of modesty, in blankets. Angelo can probably get off saying he was there professionally, but what are you going to say?"

"Spruce Harbor Flying Service announces the immediate departure of Flight Six to Boston," Wrong Way replied. "You drive a hard bargain, Hawkeye."

"It's a warming experience to know that your friends are always willing to do you a favor when you need one," Hawkeye replied.

When he returned to the sitting room, Boris and Trapper were gone. He knew immediately where they would be, and there he found them.

"I hate to be stuffy about this," Hawkeye said, "but Trapper John is only a special guest, and not allowed in here."

"I thought this was a special circumstance," Trapper said.

"Shame on you!" Boris said to him. "You just get out of here. Miss Bazoom is about to perform."

"I'll go with him, to make sure he doesn't sneak in again," Hawkeye said. "You got enough to drink, Boris, to last through the performance?"

"I don't know," Boris replied, holding up a half gallon bottle of Old White Stagg in each hand. "But if I run dry, I'll yell for more."

Outside the theater, Trapper asked. "How's it going?"

"We're all set," Hawkeye replied. "Is he going to be out before long?" "I hope so," Trapper said. "And just to make sure, I added a little something to the booze. But I've been thinking. Isn't it a dirty trick to knock him out and carry him off unconscious to dump him in the deep woods?"

"All right, we'll call the whole thing off and take him home with us," Hawkeye said. "To your house, since it's your idea."

Trapper John took a small white bottle from his pocket. "I only had one bottle of this stuff," he said. "I wonder if it's enough?"

"I think it'll be enough," Hawkeye said. "I took the precaution of putting a few drops of my own in before I sent the bottles into the sitting room."

At that point, there came the sound of a round of applause as Miss Bonnie Bazoom (and presumably her replacement pigeons) came onto the stage. This was followed by a horrible crashing noise as if someone had gotten to his feet and applauded and then collapsed, as if drugged.

Hawkeye peered into the theater and then motioned for Trapper John to follow him. In a moment, puffing and wheezing, one healer to each leg, they dragged Boris, who wore a smile on his face, out of the room.

"That does it," Trapper said, breathing heavily, after they finally propped Boris against the wall under a 60 x 48 Augustus John oil portrait of a long-forgotten Framingham Fellow. "I knew this wouldn't work. How do you propose to get him from here to the airplane?"

"You underestimate me, Doctor," Hawkeye said, gesturing toward the staircase, up which bounded four muscular young men in green nylon tunics. "Here come the cheery chaps from Tranquil Glades."*

"My apologies," Trapper said. "I should have known you could be counted on in a pinch."

"We are going to take this gentleman to the seaplane terminal at Boston Harbor," Hawkeye ordered, regally. "And place him aboard Flight Six of the Spruce Harbor Flying Service. Strap him to the stretcher, men, and we're off!"

---

* The Tranquil Glades Health Farm and Alcoholic Rehabilitation Center had had a long and mutually beneficial relationship with the Framingham Foundation and its fellows. Mr. Korsky-Rimsakov was only the last of a long line of fellows who had to be transported in an unconscious condition from foundation headquarters with great discretion.

Chapter Eight

Wrong Way Napolitano, pilot in command of Spruce Harbor Flying Service's Flight Six (one-class Beaver service to Boston and points north), to the considerable surprise of his brother Angelo, found Boston Harbor on the first try.

With a tremor of justifiable pride in his voice (on previous occasions, while seeking Boston Harbor, he had landed on such diverse bodies of water as Lake Winnipesaukee, New Hampshire, and the Leonia, New Jersey, Municipal Reservoir), Wrong Way turned in his seat and announced:

"Spruce Harbor Flying Service announces the arrival of Flight Six at Boston, Massachusetts. Please remain in your seats until the aircraft stops moving."

"Boston?" one of the passengers, a tall, lanky blond in a beehive hairdo replied. "Thank God! For a while there, Wes-Baby, you really had me going. I really thought we were actually going out in the woods."

"Shut up, you dumb broad," Wesley St. James said, rousing himself from slumber. He leaned forward in his seat and addressed the aircraft commander in high, piercing, angry-canary-like tones: "Boston? What the hell do you mean, Boston?"

"Boston, Massachusetts," Wrong Way replied.

"Wesley," Don Rhotten (who was, of course, traveling incognito as Mr. John Smith) asked, "are we on the ground? Can I open my eyes?"

"I asked you," Wesley St. James (who had decided to shun public adulation himself and was using his real name, Wladislaw Synjowlski) shouted in Wrong Way's ear, "what the hell are we doing in Boston? Where the hell is that unspoiled, crystal-clear jewel of a lake I'm paying for?"

Angelo Napolitano, who had chosen to use the *nom de guide* of Pierre LeGrande in order to conceal his close association with the proprietor of the Spruce Harbor Flying Service, put on his best French-Canadian accent and replied.

"*M'sieu*," he said, "eet is zee code of zee deep woods."

Wesley St. James had never been close to a deep Maine woods guide before. He realized there was a lot about things up here he didn't know.

"What's the code of the deep woods?" he asked.

"When a bush pilot is asked for help," Angelo replied, momentarily forgetting the French-Canadian accent, "zee code of zee deep woods requires zat he give zee help."

"To hell with that," Wesley St. James said. "I'm paying for the airplane."

"It is zee code of zee woods, *M'sieu*," Angelo said.

"What kind of help?" Wesley asked.

Wrong Way had told Angelo very little of why they were making a passenger pickup in Boston, only that "I got to ferry some stiff for Hawkeye." Angelo, like most practitioners of the legal profession, was highly skilled in taking one little fact and embellishing it somewhat.

"Once a man has spent some time in zee deep woods, *M'sieu*," Angelo said, "it is burned on his soul."

"Get to the bottom line, Pierre," Wesley St. James said. "Spare me the sales talk."

"We are returning, *M'sieu*," Angelo said, "the body of a man who once knew zee deep woods but was forced to leave zem. He asked that he be buried in zee deep woods, under zee spreading boughs of a large tree."

"What you're telling me, in other words," Wesley St. James said, "is that we're giving some corpse a free ride on my chartered airplane?"

"It is zee code of the deep woods, *M'sieu*," Angelo said, with what he thought was a splendid Gallic shrug.

"Corpse?" Don Rhotten asked. "Is that 'corpse,' as in 'dead person'?"

"So Frenchie says," Wesley St. James replied, nodding at Angelo.

"Wes, I'm afraid of dead people," Don Rhotten said. "They're . . . they're . . . *icky!*"

"Shut up, Don," Wesley St. James said. "I'm thinking."

"About what?" Don Rhotten asked. "You're not actually going to let these awful people put a dead body in here with television's most beloved young newscaster, are you?"

"I told you to shut up, Don," Wesley said. "I think I'm onto something."

"Onto what?" Don said. "Maybe Seymour was right after all. I should never have come with you. You didn't say anything about dead people, Little Bunny, you know you didn't. All you talked about was getting off alone in the woods with a couple of bimbos."

"Who are you calling a bimbo, skinhead?" the second of the female passengers, Miss LaVerne Schultz, replied angrily.

"I think," the blond, whose name was Louella Frump, said, "that you're just *awful*, Mr. Synjowlski."

"Who cares what you think, you dumb . . . wait a minute," Wesley St. James replied. "Why am I awful?"

"You have no understanding at *all!*" Louella Frump said.

"Don't you say anything like that to Little Bunny!" Don Rhotten rose to his friend's defense.

"Shut up, Don," Wesley St. James said. "Understanding about what?"

"That code of the deep woods Mr. LeGrande is talking about," she said. "That's something fine and noble, and you don't understand it at all. You have no feelings, Mr. Synjowlski!"

"You really think so, huh?" Wesley St. James said, obviously pleased.

"I really think so," she said.

"That code of the deep woods really gets to you, huh?" Wesley St. James pursued. "Right in the gut?"

"It makes me want to cry," she said.

"She's a corpse freak, that's what she is!" Don Rhotten said. "My God! What am I doing going into the deep woods with a corpse freak?"

"Shut up, Don," Wesley said. "I'm thinking."

The Beaver, which is what the technical aviation magazines refer to as a single-engine, high-wing, eight-place monoplane, had meanwhile taxied up to the seaplane terminal dock.

Wrong Way turned around again. "Ladies and gentlemen," he said, "you're going to have to move to the right side of the airplane so we can get the body in here."

"Wesley!" Don Rhotten cried, shielding his eyes with his hands. "Do something!"

"Shut up, Don," Wesley St. James said.

It was a good thing that Mr. Rhotten shielded his eyes. Otherwise, he would have seen Dr. Benjamin Franklin Pierce and Dr. John Francis Xavier McIntyre supervising the loading of Boris "on his stretcher" onto the aircraft.

Mr. Rhotten had met Drs. Pierce and McIntyre several times before, and the memory was quite painful to him.* Had he seen them at the seaplane terminal dock in Boston Harbor, the odds are that he would have gone off the deep end right there. But, with his hands over his eyes and his head cradled on the more than adequate bosom of Miss LaVerne Schultz, he saw nothing at all.

The muscular attendants from Tranquil Glades slid the stretcher, with Boris strapped to it, into the aircraft and then closed the door.

Wesley St. James and Miss Louella Frump stared in

---

* The somewhat sordid details of their first encounter are recorded in an otherwise delightful, enriching tome, M*A*S*H GOES TO MOROCCO (Pocket Books, New York, 1975).

horrified fascination at the grayish skin of the body on the stretcher.

"Don't you people," Wesley St. James finally asked, in a nervous chirp, "cover the faces of dead people? I mean, isn't that the way it's done up here?"

Boris moaned. He was reliving in his tortured dreams the shame he had experienced on the stage of the opera. The moan was piteous, and a tear rolled down his freshly shaven cheeks.

"My God!" Miss Louella Frump said. "It's alive!"

"Hey, Frenchie," Wesley St. James chirped at Angelo, alias Pierre LeGrande, "I thought you said it was a stiff?"

Angelo turned around in his seat, saw the tear, heard another moan, and saw the chest move in rhythmic breathing.

"M'sieu," he said, thinking quickly, "has misunderstood me. Pierre zay zat zee man go home to zee woods to die." He paused and then repeated, "It is zee code of zee deep woods, *M'sieu.*"

"Yeah," Wesley St. James said, thoughtfully, "the code of the deep woods." Then he turned to Miss Frump. "Say, sweetie," he said, "there'd be more room in here if I sat on your lap. How 'bout it?"

Without waiting for a reply, he climbed onto her lap. Miss Frump didn't object. In fact, she smiled. She smiled right at Pierre LeGrande, and then her right eyelid, which had been tinted with a color known as Passionate Purple, snapped closed and open in a wink. Pierre LeGrande, blushing furiously, turned around in his seat.

"I just can't wait, now," Miss Frump said, reaching out to toy with the hair at the back of Angelo's neck, "to get to the deep woods!"

Two hours later, Spruce Harbor Flying Service's Flight Six landed on Lake Kelly. Wrong Way taxied the Beaver close to shore.

"Now what?" Wesley St. James asked.

Angelo not only had no idea where they were, he didn't know what was about to happen. So he turned

93

in his seat, put his finger to his lips to signify silence and said:

"M'sieu, zis is zee sacred moment. Say nothing."

"My God!" Don Rhotten said in alarm. "There's an elephant in the bushes!"

"Don't be ridiculous, Don," Wesley St. James said. "There's no elephants in the Maine woods."

"Then you tell me what's bending those trees and making all that noise!" Don replied, somewhat hysterically.

At that moment, pushing large saplings out of his way, State Trooper Steven J. Harris appeared at the water's edge. With a mighty bound, he jumped from the shore onto the Beaver's floats. The Beaver sagged on one side. Harris was an impressive-looking law-enforcement officer, with his Smokey-the-Bear hat, Sam Browne belt, enormous Smith and Wesson .357 Magnum pistol, tunic, and glistening boots. He was also the largest and ugliest human being that Wesley St. James had ever seen, with the possible exception of the stiff on the stretcher.

"Jesus H. Christ! Who . . . or what . . . is that?" Mr. St. James inquired.

"Zat," Pierre LeGrande said, "is zee law of zee deep woods!"

Harris pulled on the door.

"Wrong Way," he said, "Angelo. This the guy Hawkeye sent me?"

"That's him," Wrong Way replied.

Trooper Harris, with professional gestures, took a stethoscope from the pocket of his tunic, placed it on Boris' chest, and listened to his heart. He took his pulse and then replaced the stethoscope. Then he unfastened the straps that bound Boris to the stretcher and, with no apparent effort whatever, pulled Boris from the stretcher and draped him over his shoulder.

"Excuse me, Mr. Policeman, sir," Wesley St. James asked. "Is he dead?"

"Oh, no," Trooper Harris replied, with a smile. "I'll have him up and around in no time."

"Is that so?" Wesley St. James asked. "You know about things like that?"

"Yes, sir," Trooper Harris replied, politely. "You see, sir, there's no doctors up here. The law has to fill in where needed."

"I'll be goddamned!" Wesley St. James said.

"I would consider it a personal favor, sir, if you would not use profanity and/or naughty words in the presence of ladies," Trooper Harris said, sternly.

"Yes, sir," Wesley St. James said. "I apologize, ladies. I don't know what came over me. Please accept my most humble and abject apologies!"

"He's *darling!*" Louella Frump said. "I don't think I have ever seen a more *darling* cop, and God knows, I've seen enough cops."

Trooper Harris blushed mightily.

"Tell Hawkeye I'll give him a call later tonight," he said to Wrong Way. And then, effortlessly, with Boris draped over his shoulder, he jumped from the Beaver's floats back onto shore. He paused at the water's edge, turned and waved, and then plunged into the deep woods.

"Did that great big ape say 'Hawkeye'?" Don Rhotten asked. "Or has my mind already cracked under the strain?"

"Shut up, Don," Wesley St. James said.

"He was not either a great big ape," Miss LaVerne Schultz said to Mr. Rhotten. "He was a great big pussycat, that's what he was!"

"Wasn't he?" Miss Frump replied, sort of cooing.

"Well," Don Rhotten sniffed, "if you ladies think he's so hot, why don't you just jump off here and go after him?"

"Shut up, Don," Wesley St. James said.

"Don't tempt me, baldy," Miss LaVerne Schultz said.

The issue was resolved when Wrong Way closed the door and shoved the throttle forward, and the Beaver turned away from the shore, gathered speed, and took off again. They flew for another forty-five minutes, twisting and turning, climbing and descending, and for the last ten minutes flying just above the treetops.

The low-level flight was necessary. The Spruce Harbor Flying and Deep Maine Woods Guide Service had promised Mr. Wladislaw Synjowlski and Mr. John Smith an unspoiled, crystal-clear lake far from the noise and hubbub of civilization. If Wrong Way had flown the airplane any higher than two-hundred feet, the passengers would have been able to see that Lost Crystal Lake was about two miles, as the crow flies, from the wide concrete band of Interstate 95 and just over a small hill from a potato chip factory operated by one of Maine's solons in the Senate.

Wrong Way taxied to the extreme north end of the lake and cut the engine. An inflatable rubber boat was tossed out the door and blown up. With Pierre LeGrande paddling enthusiastically, if somewhat unskillfully, the party of nature lovers was ferried to the shore, followed by their supplies.

They stood on the shore and watched as Wrong Way took off again.

Wesley St. James sniffed and then sniffed again.

"Hey, Frenchie," he asked, "what's that awful smell?"

"What awful smell is zat, *M'sieu?*"

"It smells like rotten potatoes."

"Zat, *M'sieu,*" Pierre LeGrande replied with grand Gallic hauteur, "zat is zee smell of zee deep woods."

"It smells like rotten potatoes to me," Don Rhotten said.

"Shut up, Don," Wesley St. James said. "What do you know?"

"Yeah," Miss LaVerne Schultz said. "Who are you, baldy, to question the word of Pierre LeGrande?" She winked at Angelo again. He hurriedly bent over a crate of supplies.

Wesley St. James walked to the edge of the water. He leaned on a tree and inhaled deeply. A smile came to his lips, a look of near ecstasy. He was glad that he'd given in to the impulse to come to the deep woods. He already had been inspired. A whole new vista of program ideas was beginning to form in his mind. The details were a little vague so far, but things would become clear in time. He wasn't known as the Napoleon of Daytime Drama for nothing.

The cold truth is that when Wesley St. James left California for New York, he was not entirely motivated by an all-consuming desire to see Big Bunny and Uncle Ralph. The truth of the matter was that he was having a couple of problems, the solutions for which at the moment evaded him.

Long ago, he had come to realize that when one is faced with a problem for which one has no answer, the prudent thing to do is make oneself scarce. He didn't think that these problems would pursue him into the deep Maine woods, although he was by no means sure of this.

Problem Number One was an actress, or rather *the* actress, Patience Throckbottom Worthington. Patience, to tell the truth, had been bugging him for a long time, since shortly after he had signed her to an exclusive seven-year contract with Wesley St. James Productions. At the time, he thought it had been a coup, a feather in his cap. Only six months before, he had been marching up and down State Street in Chicago, surrounded by sheets of plywood extolling the merits of Casimir Czylowski's Old Pinsk Polish Sausage, and now here he was signing up one of America's, indeed the world's, most distinguished actresses.

Throckbottoms and Worthingtons had trod the boards at Stratford-on-Avon, or so everybody believed, with William Shakespeare. Patience had inherited from her father, Benjamin Worthington, the famous Worthington profile. From her mother, Eleanor Culpepper Throckbottom, had come the famous Throckbottom eyes and soft, quivering speech. From both of them she had inherited not only a classical actor's manner of speech but also an affinity for the grape that had to be paid for to be believed.

In the belief he was picking up the tab for some cold chicken and a couple of bottles of wine, Wesley St. James had approved a paragraph in her contract which stipulated that "while on the set, Miss Worthington will be provided with such meals as may be necessary, provided by a caterer satisfactory to Miss Worthington, and including such wines and spirits as she may feel appropriate."

Certainly, he had figured, keeping Miss Patience T. Worthington in the best possible frame of mind was worth the price of a catered lunch and a bottle of wine. He believed (as it turned out, correctly) that Miss Patience T. Worthington would lend an aura of class to "Life's Little Agonies" that no other daytime drama could hope to match. Her dignified, warm (some said "saintly") features were world famous. Her cultured, gentle voice (she has for thirty years read " 'Twas The Night Before Christmas" on Christmas Eve to a television audience numbering over 100 million) was nearly as well known as her soft eyes and gently curled silver-white locks.

"If she wants a bottle and a bird," Wesley St. James had announced, "Wesley St. James will be honored to make them available to her."

Wesley first cast Miss Worthington as kindly Mother Howard, a role in which she had ample opportunity to gather various deeply troubled members of the cast to her breast, to comfort them, and to send them off to face philandering husbands, drunken wives, lecherous doctors, embezzling accountants, and crooked lawyers ad infinitum with the strength that comes from wisdom and godly purpose.

Wesley had, to tell the truth, been rather surprised when Miss Worthington showed up the first day on Sound Stage Three accompanied by a house trailer.

"You, theah, you dahling little man," she said, pointing at him. "Take care of the truck driver, will you?"

He knew now that he should have put his foot down right there and not only refused to pay the truck driver for hauling the trailer but barred the house trailer itself from the set. At the time, however, he had thought that since she was a big star, she would naturally have a big dressing room. Certainly, Miss Patience Throckbottom Worthington would not actually *live* in a house trailer, like ordinary mortals; it had to be a dressing room.

He had had no way of knowing, of course, that "Bird's Nest," the world-famous Worthington "cottage" overlooking the Pacific, all thirty-six rooms of it, had long since been sold for nonpayment of taxes and that the trailer in which Miss Worthington arrived on the set represented to her a considerable step upward from the Volkswagen bus in which she had for the past two years, "between engagements," been living. He learned this only three weeks later, when the Hollywood Mobile Home Company sent him a bill for the trailer. It was only then that he took another look at the contract and found the clause in which he had agreed to provide the actress "with a suitable dressing room [or trailer] of her choice, said dressing room to become the property of Miss Worthington upon completion of her engagement."

Wesley St. James, in the quaint cant of the trade, had been "schnockered" by the contract, for there was still another provision in the contract which read that "in the case of unresolvable artistic disagreement between the artist and the producer, it is agreed that Miss Worthington will be released from any obligations under this contract and that the producer will pay, in cash and in full, immediately upon demand, all sums of money which would have been paid to Miss Worthington had there been no disagreements over the life of the contract."

In other words, he could fire her, but he would have to pay her.

A lesser man would have either caved in or gone crazy, but Wesley St. James was not on his way to becoming the Napoleon of Daytime Drama without a certain stiff backbone of his own.

What saved their relationship was the simple fact that Patience Throckbottom Worthington was congenitally

99

unable to give a bad performance. It didn't matter if she had to be dragged from the trailer to the set, propped on her feet, and pushed before the cameras, to stand there bleary-eyed and weaving. Once the words "Action, lights, roll 'em" were heard, a remarkable transformation took place. Miss Worthington straightened, symbolically tossed the bottle of whatever she happened to be drinking out of camera range, shook herself, and began to emote.

Chapter Nine

Kindly Mother Howard was an instant success. Within two weeks it was necessary to hire six stenographers to reply to her fan mail, most of which sought advice for the most intimate of family problems. Wesley St. James read the most interesting of the letters and turned over the best of what he read to his writers, who incorporated the fans' problems into the scripts of "Life's Little Agonies," giving it a realism that was frequently cited as the reason for its success.

Soon, although he never quite grew accustomed to being referred to as "bleeping little four-eyed blap" by Miss Worthington, Wesley St. James came to understand that he was still getting the best of the bargain, even taking into consideration the fact that Miss Worthington and her circle of friends could consume champagne, twelve-year-old Scotch, roast pheasant, and pâté de foie gras nearly as fast as the Beverly Hills Gourmet Eppes-Essen's fleet of Buick station wagons could deliver it to the set.

Within a matter of months, in fact, Wesley St. James came to understand that the phrase "Patience Throckmorton Worthington would rather act than eat" was more than a press agent's imaginative little gem. She really would rather act than eat. Since when she was not acting she was eating (and drinking), the obvious thing to do was give her more roles. That would not only cut down on the bills from the Beverly Hills Gourmet Eppes-Essen but would, additionally, get more work out of her for the same price.

Soon, Miss Worthington, in addition to dispensing motherly advice as kindly Mother Howard on "Life's Little Agonies," was dispensing sisterly advice (as good Sister Beth) on "The Globe Spinneth"; quasi-religious advice (as Sister Piety, a nun of unspecified religious affiliation) on "Guiding Torch"; medical advice (as Nurse Jones) on "One Life to Love"; and neighborly advice (as Mrs. Olson, the lady-next-door) to the one-legged mother of three illegitimate children on "All These Children."

She was so good, in fact, that Wesley St. James, whenever he could spare the time, actually went to the sound stages to watch her work. Normally, he stayed as far away from actors and actresses as he could.

He was on the set, in fact, the day Miss Worthington dropped her bomb.

He had entered the set itself through a private door and climbed high into the flies, so that his presence would not be known to anyone but the grips and other technicians who work high over the set.

It was a scene from "Guiding Torch," the very popular daytime drama that asked the question if a man of the cloth could find happiness in being simultaneously king of the pulpit and queen of the closet.

Wesley St. James was glad that no one could see him, for his eyes misted over as Sister Piety (Miss Worthington) laid a gentle hand on the shoulder of the Reverend Bobbin (Mr. C. Walton Cowpens) and assured him that God still loved him, even if the police were about to come and ask some rather embarrassing questions about what he had been doing in the men's room at the YMCA with the junior high school boys' soccer team.

"God loves each of us," Miss Worthington/Sister Piety said. "No matter how weak we are."

"Oh, thank you, Sister Piety," the Reverend Bobbin replied, "for your kind and gentle understanding."

"Feel free to come to me whenever you need me," Sister Piety replied.

A tear ran down Wesley St. James's cheeks.

"Cut," the director called. "Print it. First class, Miss Worthington, thank you very much."

"It's about bleeping time," Miss Worthington replied. "I'm not used to having to make four bleeping takes, you bleeping jackass."

"But wasn't it worth it, Miss Worthington?" the actor who played the Reverend Bobbin inquired. "I really felt that scene." He grabbed for her hand.

"Keep your bleeping paws off me, you bleeping faggot," Miss Worthington said. "You make my bleeping skin crawl!"

"She didn't really mean that," the director said, trying to pour oil on soon-to-be troubled waters.

"The bleep I didn't," Miss Worthington replied. "And just who the bleep do you think you are, you bleeping ignoramus, to tell this bleeping no-talent blap what Patience T. Worthington means?"

"No offense, Miss Worthington," the director said, quickly.

"Where's the little blap?" Miss Worthington asked.

"Who do you mean, Miss Worthington?" the director asked.

"How bleeping many little blaps have you got?" she asked, as she swept grandly off the set toward her trailer. "The bleeping four-eyed little blap, the one with that silly bleeping haircut, that's who I mean."

"Do you mean Mr. Wesley St. James, Miss Worthington?"

"That's the one," she said. "I never can remember that silly bleeping name. Tell him I want to see him, and now."

"I'm not sure that Mr. St. James is available, Miss Worthington. He might not be in the studio."

"In that case, you stupid blat, you better bleeping well send for him," Miss Worthington said. She jerked the door of her trailer, stepped inside, and slammed it closed.

Five minutes later, after first having hastily procured a dozen long-stemmed red roses and a half-gallon bottle of Miss Worthington's favorite digestive, Old White Stagg Blended Kentucky Bourbon, Wesley St. James marched up to Miss Worthington's trailer and, after a moment's hesitation, knocked.

The door was flung open a moment later.

Miss Worthington had not yet removed her costume; she was still dressed as Sister Piety.

"Why," she cooed, her hands folded in front of her, as if in prayer, "if it isn't Mr. St. James!"

"Good afternoon, Miss Worthington," Wesley said.

"Isn't this a coincidence!" Miss Worthington replied. "I was just a moment ago thinking how nice it would be if you could spare a minute or two from your busy schedule to have a little chat with me. And then, here you are."

Wesley bobbed his head. Miss Worthington snatched the bottle of Old White Stagg from his hands. "For me? How sweet of you, you dahling man! Just the right thing for a little pick-me-up. Please come in, dear Mr. St. James, and have a drop with me!"

"Thank you," Wesley said. He was sweating profusely. He had been associated with Miss Worthington long enough to know that when she simply oozed charm and grace, she wanted something.

Miss Worthington poured four fingers of Old White Stagg into a glass, downed it, smacked her lips in pleasure, and then refilled the glass.

"That's the real thing," she said. "You really know the way to a girl's heart, don't you, you old rogue?"

Wesley St. James blushed but immediately regained control of himself.

"Is there any way at all, any way at all, in which I might be of some service to you, dear lady?" he asked. "Your happiness means a great deal to everyone at St. James Productions."

"Yes, darling, I know," Miss Worthington said. "I read those bleeping rating reports, too. And since you have brought it up, darling, there is."

"How may I be of service?" Wesley asked. Miss Worthington reached out and pinched Wesley St. James's cheek.

"Aren't you sweet?" she asked.

She turned away from him, filled her glass again, walked to the couch, hoisted her nun's robes up above her knees, and placed her feet on the coffee table.

"Here's the bottom line, Wes," she said. "Mother wants her own show."

"I see," Wesley St. James said.

"I mean, Wesley-Baby, here I am, Patience Throckbottom Worthington, grande dame of the theater, superstar of motion pictures, playing bleeping second banana to a bunch of bleeping no-talent blaps on the bleeping boob tube. Now I ask you, you're a fair man, is that bleeping fair?"

"You have raised an interesting question," Wesley St. James said.

"I knew you'd understand, you darling man," she said. "Just looking at you, one can tell that you're of the theater. Grand Guignol, perhaps, but the theater."

"Thank you, Miss Worthington," Wesley St. James replied.

"No hurry," she said, grandly. "I understand that it will take some time to develop a vehicle in which my humble talents may be most advantageously displayed. Get back to me within two weeks, Babykins, O.K.?"

"Well . . ."

"I know what you're going to say," Patience said, in her familiar, soft, refined tones.

"You do?"

"You're going to say that hardly gives you enough time."

"I *was* thinking along those lines, Miss Worthington," Wesley said.

"And you know what I'm going to reply to that?" she asked. She didn't wait for a reply but went right on. "I'm going to tell you that two bleeping weeks is all the bleeping time you get, dahling. Mother has been patient as long as Mother intends to be patient. You either come up with something, dahling, or else!"

"I see your point," Wesley said.

"You bleeping well better see it, dahling," Patience said, and then she took pity on him. "Here, have a little snort. You look a little pale."

She had him, Wesley realized, in the apt vernacular of the profession, by the short hairs. He might be the Napoleon of Daytime Drama, but there were Wellingtons in the business, too, filthy, rotten, no-good, characterless creeps who would like nothing better than to steal Patience T. Worthington away from St. James Productions, just as he had stolen C. Walton Cowpens away from Magnum Op Productions to play the Reverend Bobbins.

In the following two weeks, the writers of St. James Productions came up with no less than seventeen different ideas for a daytime drama starring Miss Worthington. None of them, in Miss Worthington's succinct phraseology, "were worth a blap."

"Wesley, dahling," Miss Worthington had telephoned him to say, "I hate to tell you this, precious, but you're becoming a bleeping disappointment. I'll give you one more week, and that's it!"

"Not to worry, Miss Worthington," Wesley had replied. "I'm flying to the East Coast this very afternoon to confer with someone who will, I'm sure, come up with something suitable."

"He bleeping well better," she had replied and hung up.

That was problem Number One. Problem Number Two was also an actress, this one named Zelda Spinopolous, who had chosen (more precisely, whose mother had chosen) the professional name Daphne Covington. Mrs. Spinopolous was a typical stage mother, with one major exception. Like most stage mothers, Mrs. Spinopolous had had an interrupted theatrical career and was determined to experience a vicarious show business success through her daughter. Mrs. Spinopolous, in her young womanhood, had been the third high kicker from the left in the second row of the Corps de Ballet of Sidney Katz's Maison de Paris in Cicero, Illinois.

Had she not entered the bonds of holy matrimony with Mr. Gustaphalous "Gus" Spinopolous, as she often reminded Mr. Spinopolous, there was just no telling how far, how high she might have traveled in what she chose to call "the world of theater." The fruit of their union was educated by her mother in the theatrical arts from the time she first toddled erect across the living room carpet. There had been tap dance lessons, ballet lessons, and elocution lessons, and the child had been exposed to the theatrical world at every opportunity.

Mr. Spinopolous, who wasn't, frankly, too anxious to see his only child become a world-famous star and would have much preferred that she find some nice Greek Orthodox boy whom he might bring into the business/ and with whom she could make him a grandfather, only put his foot down once. It was entirely possible, he said, that Zelda might not wish to be a world-famous star, and in that case she would need a good education. He would make his wife a little proposition. If she laid off Zelda while Zelda attended the University of Chicago, he would "do what he could" to get her a chance in show business when she had graduated.

It was his belief that Zelda would be diverted from the path her mother had laid out for her by a young man. The young man would march her to the altar, come into the business, and make him a grandfather, and what he privately thought of as "this movie star crap" would be forgotten.

To her father's delight and her mother's bafflement (what possible use would a movie star have for a degree in analytic biology?), Zelda spent five years at the University of Chicago, deeply enmeshed in her studies. There were, however, no young men in her life. Her father believed this to be because Zelda was a good girl and knew she was too good for those unshaven bums and general all around ne'er-do-wells who obviously dominated the student body. Her mother believed her lack of apparent interest in the opposite gender was because Zelda was saving herself for the dashing and handsome young men who would gather at her feet once she had climbed the glittering staircase to stardom.

The truth was that Zelda was regarded as something of a bore by the young gentlemen of her acquaintance, mainly because they did not share her fascination with protozoa, baccili, and germ cultures. The feeling was somewhat reciprocal. Zelda had learned early on that she really preferred to spend her evenings with her microscope to spending them standing around a smoke-filled apartment with a limp shrimp in one hand a lukewarm bottle of Dr Pepper in the other, conserving her strength for the wrestling match that invariably followed. Zelda was possessed of a frame that inflamed the reproductive urges of young male *homo sapiens*. While Zelda-the-Biologist understood this as a perfectly natural, indeed essential, portion of the life cycle, Zelda Spinopolous was not quite ready, as she thought of it, for fertilization.* Consequently, her dates grew less and less frequent, until they finally disappeared altogether from her social calendar.

The Biology vs. the Theater controversy came to a head following Zelda's graduation as B.S. (cum laude) and M.S. (summa cum laude) and her announcement that, if it was all right with Mommy and Daddy, she would just remain in school and shoot for her Ph.D.

It was not all right with Mommy and Daddy. Mommy announced, somewhat hysterically, that unless Zelda began her career right now, all she could hope to be was a character actress, and she, Bonita Granville Spinopolous, had no intention whatever of being known as a character actress' mother.

Then she threw a Chef Pierre frozen New England

---

* Biologists and botanists place different meaning on the term "fertilization." To botanists it implies applying some organic (or chemical) substance to the root structure of a plant; to biologists it does not. Hence the phrase "Biologists Have More Fun."

boiled dinner, aluminum tray, corned beef, soggy cabbage and all, at Mr. Spinopolous together with the announcement that it was all quite clearly his fault.

Mr. Spinopolous, who had twenty-five years before learned that the only way to deal with his wife under such circumstances was to flee, fled, taking Zelda with him. They rode around Chicago, and finally Mr. Spinopolous stopped the car overlooking Lake Michigan.

He was as disturbed as his wife by Zelda's announcement that she wanted to remain in school and become a Ph.D. He faced the bitter truth that Zelda (who was nearing twenty-four) was getting a little long in the tooth, and unless she was soon impaled with Cupid's arrow, he was liable to have an old maid on his hands.

All that he really expected from his daughter was that she bring some suitable young man home, someone to step into his shoes in the business and someone with whom his beloved Zelda could cooperate in the production of a grandchild, preferably male.

Perhaps his wife was right. Perhaps Zelda would find a man in Hollywood. That was better than nothing, and nothing was what Zelda had turned up with at the University of Chicago.

"You're going to have to plan for your future, Zelda," he said, finally.

"I know what I want, Daddy," Zelda said. "I want to be a biologist!"

"Sometimes, baby," her father said, "you don't get what you want in life. I never wanted anything out of life but to open a little restaurant, maybe with a little bar in it, and look what happened to me."

"Oh, Daddy," Zelda said. "I never knew that. You never said anything!"

"You don't complain about things you can't change, Zelda," her father said. "You just go along. I think you're gonna have to go along with your mother."

"I don't want to be an actress!"

"I didn't want to be what I am, baby," he said, "but

you learn to live with things. You try it for a year, and if you don't like it, you can go back to college. O.K.?"

They drove back to the house.

"Zelda and me talked it over, cupcake," Mr. Spinopolous said to his wife, who had, after smashing all the breakable objects in the living room in a little pique, collapsed on the couch with a bottle of gin.

"And?"

"Zelda's gonna give it a whirl for a year."

"A star is born!" Mrs. Spinopolous cried, getting somewhat unsteadily to her feet. "Watch out, Hollywood, here comes Daphne Covington!"

"Who the hell is Daphne Covington?" Gus asked.

"Who ever heard of a star with a name like Zelda Spinopolous?" Mrs. Spinopolous replied.

It was at this point that the difference between Mrs. Spinopolous and other stage mothers became apparent. The others were forced by circumstance to grovel at the feet of third-assistant second-unit directors, to fawn over women whose second cousin, once removed, had been a college roommate of an assistant producer, anything to bring their child to the attention of someone in show business who could give the kid a role.

Mrs. Spinopolous did not have this problem. On the following morning, her husband summoned into his office his advertising director and had a word with him.

He wanted, he said, to get his daughter into show business. If possible, he wanted her to get into show business, something nice, right here in Chicago, for he didn't like the idea of sweet Zelda having to go to either Hollywood, California, or New York City, which were, he had heard, hotbeds of depravity and sexual hanky-panky completely unsuited to a young lady of good Greco-Polish background.

"I'll get right back to you, chief," the advertising director said. "You got anything specific in mind?"

"I'll leave it up to you," Gus said.

The advertising manager, in the cant of the trade, got on the horn and telephoned the executive vice-president, advertiser relations, of the Amalgamated Broadcasting System in New York. The executive vice-president was candidly informed that although Zelda had had training as a child in tap, ballet, and elocution, she had absolutely zero professional experience.

"Not to worry," the executive vice-president said. "I'm sure something can be worked out. I'll get back to you." He broke the connection with his finger and then told the operator to get Mr. Wesley St. James on the West Coast hot line.

"Wes-Baby," he said, "the network's got a little ol' problem we think you can help us with."

"Such as?"

"We have to find employment for a dame."

"I understand," Wesley St. James replied. "I'll scratch your back, Fenwick, and you scratch mine later, right?"

"Let me lay it out for you," Fenwick said. "Wesley St. James Productions brings in thirty-nine and two-tenths percent of the total ABS advertising revenue, right?"

"You got it, Fenwick."

"And who is the major advertiser on Wesley St. James Productions?"

"Chef Pierre's Frozen Delights," Wesley St. James instantly replied. "They spend . . . God knows . . . *a lot of money!*"

"Right," Fenwick said.

"And do you know what would happen if Chef Pierre's Frozen Delights cancelled their advertising with us, Wes-Baby?"

"I don't know. Why would they want to do that?"

"If Chef Pierre cancelled, Wes-Baby, ABS would scratch Wesley St. James Productions. Nothing personal, of course, but that's the way the cookie would crumble."

"But why would they want to do that?"

"I think they would do it if, for example, Wesley St. James Productions couldn't find a starring role for Chef Pierre's one and only daughter."

"Is there really a Chef Pierre? I thought that was just made up."

"He's a Greek," Fenwick said, "named Gus. But that's neither here nor there, Wes-Baby, is it?"

"What does he want?"

"He wants his little girl to star in a Wesley St. James Production, something decent, Wes, I think I should mention that, and laid, you should excuse the expression, in Chicago."

"Chicago! Why Chicago? Nothing's going on in Chicago but Mayor Daly, and he's hardly what you could call boffo in the daytime drama department."

"That's what Gus wants, baby. And what Gus wants, Gus gets."

"I get your point. I'll get back to you, Fenwick."

"Quickly, Wesley. Say within a week. A nice, new show. Clean, uplifting, prestigious."

"Can this chef's daughter act?"

"Does that matter, Wesley?"

"I suppose not," Wesley St. James replied. The line went dead in his ear. He left almost immediately for New York. He needed time to think. He had been in tighter spots before; he would think his way out of this one, too.

Chapter Ten

There is, on the wall by the chief nurse's station of the Spruce Harbor Medical Center, a large device known as the doctor board. It has a more formal title, of course, something like the Handy-Dandy Executive Model Medical Professional Personnel Locator, but it has been known since its installation as the doctor board.

The name of each physician admitted to the hospital staff is listed on the board in small white letters. So are the names of the registered nurses, the pharmacists, and some other professionals in whose whereabouts at all times the hospital has an interest.

Behind each name are spaces into which little plugs are fitted as appropriate. There's a line of holes marked "IN," another line marked "OFFICE," another marked "VACATION" and a final line marked "OTHER." The final line is followed by a plastic surface on which the listee is required to write his or her whereabouts if she or he is not "IN," at the "OFFICE," or on "VACATION." To maintain a certain nose-to-the-grindstone image insofar as patients, visitors, and other nonprofessionals who can look at the board are concerned, certain euphemisms are used.

"LABORATORY," for example, meant that the listee could be found, if necessary, at Stanley K. Warczinski's Bide-a-While Pool Hall and Saloon, Inc. "DEPT. OF HEALTH" meant that the listee, armed with a weighted club, was chasing a small white ball around the links of the Spruce Harbor Country Club. "BOARD MEETING" meant that the listee was in the office of Dr. Benjamin Franklin Pierce, chief of surgery, slurping martinis and should not be summoned to the practice of medicine for anything less than a major catastrophe, in which the risk of having him apply a Band-Aid might be justified.

Three days after Spruce Harbor Flying Service's Flight Six had flown Mr. St. James and Mr. Rhotten to Lost Crystal Lake, there was quite a stir at the doctor board. Doctors and nurses from all over the Spruce Harbor Medical Center came to look at the board (to confirm with their own eyes what rumor had quickly spread throughout the hospital), shake their heads, and shrug their shoulders in complete bafflement.

It was obviously no error. The same two words were written after the names of both Dr. Pierce and his boon companion, fellow veteran of the Korean War, and partner in chest-cutting, John Francis Xavier McIntyre, M.D.

It was agreed that it was some new kind of euphemism, a really brilliant stroke, and one which would certainly add to the nose-to-the-Hippocratic-grindstone image they were all so interested in fostering. The trouble was that no one could imagine (despite some really imaginative guessing) what the euphemism really meant, For what was written after the names of Hawkeye and Trapper John was "HOUSE CALL." No one believed this, of course . . . it was tantamount to heresy . . . and everyone's curiosity was aroused. Telephone calls were made to all the watering places, golf courses, pizza stands, and other establishments to which the two healers had ever been known to repair for a brief respite from the pressures of their medical duties. Neither surgeon had been seen recently in any of them. Finally, curiosity overwhelming him, T. Alfred Crumley, Spruce Hospital Medical Center administrator (who secretly hoped that he would catch the medical gentlemen doing something he could really sock them for), telephoned Mrs. Pierce to inquire as to the whereabouts of her mate.

"All I know, Mr. Crumbum . . ." she began to reply.

"That's Crumley, Mrs. Pierce, C, R, U, M, L, E, Y," he said, spelling it for her.

"Isn't that odd? I wonder why my husband always pronounces that Crumbum?"

"I really would have no idea," Mr. Crumley said. "As you were saying?"

"All I know is that Dr. McIntyre came here carrying his medical bag, and my husband got his medical bag, and they got into Little Benjie's swamp buggy . . ."

"Into what?"

"Into the swamp buggy," she repeated. "You know, that truck thing with the big wheels?"*

"I recall the vehicle you describe," he said. "And?"

"They drove off in it, that's all I know."

"And you have no idea where they were going?"

"None at all, I'm afraid," she said. "I did hear them saying something about a smoked . . . or was it 'pickled'? . . . ham in the deep woods."

"Would you ask them to telephone me immediately, should you hear from them?" Crumley asked.

"Certainly, Mr. Crumbum . . . Oops! Sorry. Force of habit."

Mr. Crumley broke the connection without saying anything else at all.

What had happened, of course, was that Drs. Pierce and McIntyre were in fact making what no one of their professional associates was willing to believe they would make, a house (more accurately, a log-cabin) call. They drove up Interstate 95 for about forty-five minutes and then left the superhighway through a gate marked NO EGRESS FOR UNOFFICIAL VEHICLES.

"What do you suppose that sign means?" Hawkeye, who was driving, asked.

"I have no idea what an egress is," Trapper said, "but

---

* The swamp buggy, a trucklike object with enormous wheels, had been the nativity gift to the infant B. F. Pierce of Colonel Jean-Pierre de la Chevaux. The details surrounding the incident have been superbly related in M*A*S*H GOES TO NEW ORLEANS (Pocket Books, New York, 1975).

'not to worry. My bride packed a lunch. We won't need any egresses anyway."

"Besides," Hawkeye said, "this is not an unofficial vehicle. This is an official de la Chevaux Petroleum Corporation swamp buggy."

They plunged through pine forests and swamps and finally emerged on the far shore of Lake Kelly. The vehicle drove right off the shore into the lake and then, sending enormous plumes of water into the sky from its huge tires, proceeded to sort of swim across.

"Dr. Smith doesn't expect us," Trapper said. "Have you thought about that?"

"Well, perhaps he'll be able to squeeze us in," Hawkeye said. "Now that he's temporarily given up his obstetrical and surgical practice."

"It fits all right with your sense of medical ethics that he practice psychiatry?"

"He's not really *practicing* psychiatry," Hawkeye said. "It's more on the order of being a male practical nurse."

"My God," Trapper said. "Smell that!"

Hawkeye dutifully sniffed.

"Well, I'll tell you one thing," he said. "That's not the senator's potato chip operation."

"Not unless some miracle has been worked," Trapper said. "That really makes my mouth water."

The smell grew stronger and even more appetizing during the next ten minutes, as the swamp buggy crossed the lake and crawled ashore beside a log cabin. Hawkeye sounded the air horn, which played the first six bars of the Colonel Bogie March, and then shut the swamp buggy's diesel engine down.

State Trooper Steven J. Harris emerged from the log cabin.

"You're just in time for lunch," he said.

"The sign said we couldn't have any egress," Trapper replied. "Is that roast egress I smell?"

"It's roast venison," Harris said. "That guy you sent me can really cook. You're in for a treat."

"How is he?" Hawkeye asked.

"Happy as a pig in mud," Harris replied. "He seems to really like it out here. He's been cutting wood. And cooking. And telling me stories." Harris winked. "You really should hear his stories."

"Where is he?" Trapper John asked.

Harris nodded over his shoulder. Boris, wearing a wool plaid shirt and canvas trousers, over which was a white apron, came out of the cabin carrying a large Dutch oven.

"How they hanging, Boris?" Trapper called.

"Hiya, fellas," Boris said jovially. "Glad to see you."

"What's in the pot?" Hawkeye asked.

"Venison sauerbraten," Boris replied. "Steve said he never had any venison sauerbraten."

"Neither have I," Hawkeye said.

"You'll like it, even with that peasant's palate of yours. Karajan's chef taught me the secret. I was singing Tanhäuser at the Vienna State Opera at the time, and since I obviously didn't have to rehearse to sing that, I had some time on my hands. I naturally put it to good use."

Trooper Harris winked at Hawkeye to show that he understood.

"You haven't gotten homesick for Vienna, Boris?" Hawkeye asked.

"Vienna, like Paris, will just have to suffer along without me for a while," Boris replied.

"Well, what about your friends?" Trapper asked. "Won't they miss you?"

"The only friends I have," Boris said, "excepting, of course, Hot Lips, Frenchy, and Hassan, are right here. The others are just parasites, bleeding me dry for their own selfish purposes."

"Well, what I'm saying is don't you think Hot Lips, Hassan, and Frenchy will worry about you?"

"Of course they will," Boris said. "They are probably beside themselves with concern and worry. But they'll just have to make the best of it. In due time, I shall write and explain to them why I found it necessary to temporarily turn my back on fame and fortune and to

117

spend some time in the deep woods. They'll understand. I haven't written so far, because I know the moment they know where I am, they will rush here and beg me to return to my former life."

"You don't miss the singing?" Hawkeye asked.

"I haven't stopped singing," Boris said. "I could never do that. I sing for an hour every morning, just as the sun comes up."

"You really ought to be here for that, Doctor," Trooper Harris said. "It's really something."

"You like his singing, do you, Steve?"

"Not only me," Harris said. "This morning we had two elk, a moose, and two gray wolves. It was like a choir, almost."

"And no one," Boris said, significantly, "coughed, rattled his program, or whispered to anyone else."

"Sing along with Boris, huh?" Trapper said.

"You could put it that way," Boris said. "But if you were wise, Trapper, you wouldn't."

"Where'd you get the venison this time of year?"

"I was out," Boris said, innocently, "chopping wood for the stove. I was attacked by this vicious animal and forced to defend myself."

"And we didn't want it to go to waste, of course," Trooper Harris said.

"You'll make a fine doctor," Hawkeye said to him. "You lie so easily, and so well."

"What brings you up here?" Boris asked.

"Well, we thought we'd have a look at Antoinette DeBois and her baby, and, well, since we were in the neighborhood, we thought we'd drop in and say hello," Hawkeye said.

"Well, there's more than enough to eat," Boris said. "Since you're here," he pointed an imperious finger at Trapper John, "you may help me carry the rest of the food out," he said. "We're lunching al fresco, by the side of the lake."

Hawkeye waited until Trapper and Boris were out of earshot, then spoke to Harris:

"How's it going, Steve?"

"Piece of cake," Harris replied. "Aside from those crazy stories he tells . . . God, you'd have to believe he had scored with every other woman in the world, if you believed those stories . . . he's really a very nice guy."

"And that's all he talks about?"

"No. I talk to him too. I told him . . . I hope you don't mind . . . about me wanting to go to medical school next year."

"What did he have to say about that?"

"He told me not to worry about getting in," Harris chuckled, "or about paying for it. He said that he had friends who would pay for it, and if I had any trouble getting in, he could arrange that, too. He said if nothing else, he would have his friend Hassan buy me a medical school." Harris paused. "I shouldn't be smiling, I guess. Anybody who can come up with something like that is really bananas, isn't he?"

"And he told you that he was the world's greatest opera singer?"

"Yeah," Harris said, and he was unable to keep from smiling. "He told me that in absolute confidence. He said if the word got out, they'd come looking for him and drag him back to Paris."

"I'm sure you can be trusted not to spread the word around," Hawkeye said.

"My lips are sealed. What a fantastic idea! Him being an opera singer! I thought for a while this morning that he was about to get in a butting contest with the bull elk. When the lady elk bellowed back at Boris, the bull didn't like it at all."

"There is no explaining the female taste, I suppose," Hawkeye said.

"I don't know what would have happened if the wind hadn't shifted from the direction of the potato chip factory and made the bull elk sick to his stomach," Harris said.

Boris and Trapper came back then, carrying steaming

bowls of food, and the conversation had to be cut short. Boris, however, managed to have a moment alone with Hawkeye himself. He sent Trapper and Harris to fetch the beer.

"I really have to hand it to you, Hawkeye," he said.

"For what?"

"For really being able to pick good friends."

"Like Trapper, you mean?"

"Him, too, I suppose," Boris replied. "But I was really thinking about me and Steve. He's really one hell of a guy. He's never been around much, just in the army . . . things must have changed since we were soldiers, Hawkeye. Would you believe he's a . . . don't laugh . . . virgin?"

Hawkeye didn't laugh.

"I told him that as soon as I get my feet on the ground, I'll have Esmerelda or the baroness fly over and fix that," Boris said. "But he doesn't seem interested."

"How ungrateful of him," Hawkeye said.

"He says he doesn't have time for sex and won't until he gets to be a doctor."

"The sacrifices that we healers make in the name of Hippocrates are seldom understood by the layman," Hawkeye replied, solemnly. He changed the subject. "Well, Boris, I am delighted to find that you have found peace and contentment in the deep woods," he said.

"I sometimes feel a little sorry for the Paris Opéra and my fans," Boris said. "But then I ask myself, what did they ever do for me?"

"I understand. How long do you plan to stay here?"

"A couple of weeks more," Boris said. "Maybe a month. A month without me should teach them how abysmally empty life is without me. And more time than a month would really be unnecessarily cruel."

"You're a kind man, Boris," Hawkeye said.

"I know," Boris said. "I think I'll let Hassan know first . . . say in three weeks . . . so that he can arrange my triumphant return. Perhaps with a parade down the Champs Elysées."

"At night, of course," Hawkeye said.

"Don't be silly. How could they see me at night?"

"I was thinking of fireworks, fired from the Arc de Triomphe," Hawkeye said, "and searchlights sending columns of light into the sky."

"You may have something," Boris said. "I'll think about it."

"And in the meantime, mum's the word?"

"Precisely," Boris said.

"You wouldn't want to come by the house for a couple of days?" Hawkeye asked.

"I hate to tell you this, Hawkeye," Boris said, "but that wife of yours has a big mouth. She would not be able to restrain herself from boasting before her little friends that I had favored her with a visit."

"You're probably right, Boris," Hawkeye said. "I would like to thank you for talking with me like this."

"Think nothing of it," Boris said. "But I must tell you this, Hawkeye. If it got out, via you, where I am, our friendship would be placed under a severe strain."

"I'll remember that," Hawkeye said.

"It isn't often, you know, that someone like you is in a position to do a service for someone like me. Don't blow it."

"I'll do my best."

After luncheon, which lasted two hours, Trapper John and Hawkeye got back into the swamp buggy, fired up the diesel engine, played the first six bars of the Colonel Bogie March on the air horns, and drove back into Lake Kelly. They sailed majestically down the lake, sending up huge plumes of water behind them, until they reached another log cabin on the shore.

They landed again, this time not sounding the air horn, and paid a professional visit, in the guise of a social visit, to Antoinette and Pierre DeBois and their week-old baby. Pierre DeBois, in accordance with what really was what Angelo Napolitano had called the code of the deep woods, produced a five-gallon jug of what might be called the fruit of the deep woods, and the infant, so to speak, was toasted.

The unmistakable, somewhat piquant odor of the moonshine was still about them when, two hours later, Dr. Pierce and Dr. McIntyre rolled up before the main door of the Spruce Harbor Medical Center in the swamp buggy, shut it down, and marched to the doctor board, where they changed their status from "HOUSE CALL" to "IN."

When they turned around, they faced Mr. T. Alfred Crumley, the hospital administrator, who was in the act of sniffing.

"Ah ha!" he said. "I thought so."

"You thought what, Mr. Crumbum?" Trapper John replied.

"You two have been tippling," Crumley said. "And that's Crum*ley*, Doctor. How many times must I tell you that?"

"Tell me what? That I've been tippling? I know that. I was there when I did it. We just came in to stock up."

"As hospital administrator, I have the right to know what you meant when you wrote "House Call" on the Handy-Dandy Executive Model Medical Professional Personnel Locator."

"On the what?"

"On the doctor board."

"We were making a house call," Hawkeye replied.

"All I can say to you," Mr. Crumley said, after taking a deep, injured breath and releasing it slowly through pursed lips, "is that you have a very *odd* sense of humor, if I do say so myself."

"Is there any other way we might be of some service to you, T. Alfred?" Hawkeye asked.

"There have been telephone calls for you," Mr. Crumley replied.

"Indeed?"

"If I am to believe what I strongly suspect to be persons possessed of senses of humor quite as odd as your own," T. Alfred said, consulting a sheath of little yellow slips of paper, "you are asked to call back His Royal Highness Prince Hassan of Hussid, in Paris, France; the secretary of state in Washington, D.C.; the Right Reverend Mother Emeritus of the God Is Love in All Forms Christian Church, Inc., of New Orleans, Louisiana; and a Mr. Waldo Maldemer, who described himself as 'America's Most Beloved Television Journalist' of the Amalgamated Broadcasting System in New York City."

Hawkeye took the slips from T. Alfred Crumley's hand. He turned them face down and spread them, like a deck of cards, in his hand. "Take a card," he said.

Trapper put his hands over his eyes and took two of the four slips of paper. He read them. "I got Tubby and Hot Lips," he said. "That means you lost. You got Hassan and Waldo Maldemer."

Hawkeye turned away from Mr. Crumley and to the hospital telephone operator, whose switchboard was behind the chief nurse's station.

"Sweetie,' he said, handing her all the yellow slips, "would you get all these people for us? Collect, of course. We'll be in my office."

Trapper John stepped up to the doctor board again. He moved the pegs behind his name and that of Dr. Pierce from "IN," to "IN CONFERENCE." The chief nurse spoke.

"Doctor," she said, "I couldn't help but overhear the operator. Are you going to call Hot Lips back? Could I say hello to her?"

"Right," Hawkeye said. "Come along."

"Hot Lips? Who is Hot Lips?" T. Alfred Crumley asked.

"I fear, Mr. Crumbum," Dr. Pierce said, "that you have overstepped the line. That information is classified as a medical secret."

The chief nurse went to the doctor board and moved

her peg from "IN" to "IN CONFERENCE." Over her shoulder, as the trio marched down the corridor to the office of the chief of surgery, she called out an order to the telephone operator:

"Get Hot Lips* first," she said.

---

* Lt. Col. Margaret Houlihan Wachauf Wilson, U.S. Army Nurse Corps, Retired, who had come to be known and loved as "Hot Lips Houlihan" during her service with the 4077th MASH during the Korean War, had become in later life the Right Reverend Mother Emeritus of the God Is Love in All Forms Christian Church of New Orleans, Louisiana. The details of her accession to this exalted ecclesiastical position, from those with an interest in socioreligious phenomena, may be found in M*A*S*H GOES TO NEW ORLEANS (Pocket Books, New York, 1975). Her close friendship with the chief nurse of the Spruce Harbor Medical Center began when they shared the care of His Grace, the Duke of Folkestone. The details of that touching manifestation of hands-across-the-sea have been splendidly recorded for posterity in M*A*S*H GOES TO LONDON (Pocket Books, New York, 1975).

Chapter Eleven

Dr. John Francis Xavier McIntyre, Chief Nurse Esther Flanagan, and Chief of Surgery Benjamin Franklin Pierce worked as a smoothly meshing team of experts, every motion reflecting long hours of experience. Trapper John got out the glasses and the mixing pitcher; Esther scooped both the ice from the refrigerator and the onions from their bottle; and Hawkeye, with a surgeon's sure hand and skilled eye, quickly added the right amounts, in the precise proportions, of gin and vermouth. In less time than it takes to tell about it, the trio were seated on Dr. Pierce's soft, wide couch, their feet up on the coffee table, an icy-cold martini in each of three hands.

"How's Antoinette and the boy?" Nurse Flanagan inquired.

"In splendid all-around health," Trapper John replied.

"I'll drink to that," Hawkeye said.

"You've really got Ol' Crumbum in a swivet," Flanagan said. "That 'House Call' line really drove him up the wall."

"I'll drink to that," Trapper John said.

"What's Hot Lips want?" Nurse Flanagan inquired.

"She wants to know if I know where Boris is," Hawkeye replied.

"And do you?"

"I do, but I can't tell her," Hawkeye replied. (One tells the truth and the whole truth to chief nurses. This is known as Rule Two.)

"Then you better not tell me," Flanagan replied.

(Registered nurses of long experience do not lie to each other. This is known as Rule Six.)

At that moment, the telephone on the coffee table rang. Flanagan grabbed it.

"Office of the chief of surgery," she said, crisply. "Chief of nursing services speaking." There was a reply, to which Flanagan responded by extending her lower lip in a gesture signifying that she was either impressed or that she had a piece of martini onion between her teeth and handed the telephone to Hawkeye.

"Dr. Pierce," Hawkeye said.

"This is Edgar Crudd, Doctor," a smooth, hearty male voice said. "I'm calling on behalf of America's most beloved newscaster."

"And how is Howard K. Smith these days?" Hawkeye replied.

"We don't mention *that* name around here," Crudd said, quickly. "I refer, of course, to Waldo Maldemer."

"You're not trying to tell me old droopy jowls is America's most beloved newscaster?" Hawkeye asked.

"I have to," Crudd confessed. "Waldo had that written into his contract."

"I see. Well, how may I help you, Mr. Mud?"

"That's Crudd, Doctor. Edgar *Crudd*."

"Sorry," Hawkeye said. "What's on your mind?"

"It's actually what's on Waldo's mind that I'm calling about, Doctor," Edgar Crudd said. "We have it on reliable information that you are hiding some singer named Boris A. Korsky-Rimsakov up there. Answer yes or no."

"Why do you ask?" Hawkeye replied.

"The French can't find him," Crudd said. "Say, Doc, you're not supposed to do that."

"Do what?"

"When ABS Television News calls on behalf of America's most beloved television journalist and tells you to answer yes or no, you're supposed to do that. You're not supposed to ask why we're asking."

"Well, why are you?"

"Because that's my job, that's why," Edgar Crudd said.

"We can't get everything off the news service wire, you know. Sometimes we have to ask people things."

"A little less vermouth this time, if you please," Hawkeye said.

"I beg your pardon?" Edgar Crudd said.

"Certainly," Hawkeye replied.

"Are you going to answer yes or no or not?"

"My options are up to three, I see," Hawkeye said. "Well, Mr. Fudd, it's been pleasant chatting with you this way, but my martini is getting warm." He dropped the telephone into its cradle. Almost immediately, it rang again.

Trapper John grabbed it.

"I hope this is important," he snarled into it. "We're in conference." There was a snarling sound in his ear, and then Trapper John smiled broadly. "How goes it, Hot Lips?" He covered the microphone with his hand. "It's Reverend Mother," he said.

"Let me talk to her," Nurse Flanagan said. She snatched the phone from Trapper's hands. "Margaret, how nice to hear your voice!" she said. The calling party said something, and Nurse Flanagan replied, "Oh, we're just sitting around Hawkeye's office having a little martinerooney." Pause. "Well, we wish you were here, too, dear. How's things at the nursing school?* Pause. "Well, I don't suppose you were such an angel yourself, Maggie, when you were a student nurse." Pause. "Yes, he's here, but you're wasting your time, dear. He's not going to tell you where the big ape is." She thereupon handed the telephone to Hawkeye.

"Hello, Hot Lips," Hawkeye said. "How's every little thing?" Pause. "I'm sorry, that falls into the category of doctor-patient confidentiality." Pause. "A nice right reverend mother emeritus shouldn't use words like that, Hot Lips." Pause. "Or like those, either." Pause. "I can

---

* In addition to her many responsibilities in connection with the God Is Love in All Forms Christian Church, Inc., Right Reverend Mother Emeritus Wilson also serves as chief of nursing education and guidance counseling at the Prudence MacDonald Memorial School of Nursing of New Orleans, Louisiana.

assure you, Hot Lips, that Boris is in no danger and is enjoying the best of health. I am honor bound not to reveal his whereabouts." Pause. "I understand your concern, Reverend Mother," he said, somewhat icily, "but I must tell you that I do too know what honor means. Here's Esther again."

He handed the phone back to Chief Nurse Flanagan.

"I told you he wouldn't tell you," Esther Flanagan said. Pause. "Oh, I couldn't tell him *that*. As a doctor he knows as well as you do as a nurse that it's physiologically impossible." Pause. "All I know, Maggie, is that the two of them were off all day in the swamp buggy and just came in here reeking of moonshine."

"Thanks a lot," Trapper John said.

"No more of my booze for that one," Hawkeye said. "I have apparently nurtured a viper at my gin bottle."

"I'll meet your plane," Esther Flanagan said. "And I'll see what I can find out until you get here." Pause. "I'll look forward to seeing you, too, dear." She hung the phone up.

"Flanagan, you have betrayed us!" Hawkeye said. "Or am I incorrect in assuming that the right reverend mother is about to descend upon us like an avenging angel?"

"Hawkeye," Flanagan said, "Margaret is concerned about Boris."

"She can be concerned about him just as well in New Orleans," Trapper replied. "What does she have to come here for?"

There was no chance for Trapper to force a reply out of Chief Nurse Flanagan. The telephone rang again, and she snatched it up. "Office of the chief of surgery, chief of nursing services speaking." Pause. "Why, yes, of course, I recognize your voice," she said. "Gee, to think of little ol' me talking to Harry Reasoner!" Pause. "It's not? Of course, how stupid of me. How are you today, Mr. Chancellor?" Pause. "Now listen here, whoever you are, don't you dare use language like that to me!" She handed the phone to Trapper John. "It's some dirty-mouthed old man who says he's Waldo Maldemer."

"Hello?" Trapper John said. "Is this really Waldo Maldemer?" Pause. "Well, how do I know that? You could be anyone calling up here and saying you're Waldo Maldemer." Pause. "That funny way you talk, you could be the secretary of state using words like that to a complete stranger. How can I help you, Waldo ol' pal?"

He covered the microphone with his hand. "He says it's Waldo Maldemer." Then he returned his attention to the telephone. "Odd that you should ask that question, Wado," he said. "It came up before, just a couple of minutes ago. A fellow named Fudd called . . ." Pause. "Yes, you're right. *Crudd* was his name. Well, Mr. Crudd asked the same question. Why don't you ask him what he found out?" Pause. "Well, if Edgar Crudd won't tell you, Waldo," Trapper said, "I don't think I should, either. Nice talking to you, Waldo." He dropped the phone into the cradle.

And again the phone rang immediately.

"My turn," Hawkeye said. He picked the phone up and announced, "Office of the chief nurse, chief gall bladder snatcher speaking."

"Wise guy!" Esther Flanagan snorted, momentarily diverting her attention from filling her martini glass.

"Hey, Horsey," Hawkeye went on, "how's every little thing?" He covered the mouthpiece with his hand. "It's Colonel Jean-Pierre de la Chevaux. Let's have a little quiet in here so I can hear the colonel."

Trapper, very quietly, extended his martini glass to Nurse Flanagan, who very quietly filled it.

"Why?" Hawkeye inquired. "Is he missing?" Pause. "You don't say? He ran away?" Pause. It was a very long pause, for Colonel de la Chevaux not only related in infinite detail what had happened on the stage of the Paris Opéra during the Third Act of Wagner's opera *Siegfried* but was forced to interrupt the narrative frequently as both he and Dr. Pierce chuckled, giggled, guffawed, and howled in appropriate places. But finally, as they say, the whole tale was told.

"Well, Horsey, that explains a good deal," Hawkeye said. "On your word of honor as Grand Whosis, or whatever it is, of the Bayou Perdu Council, Knights of Columbus,* that you will hold what I tell you in absolute confidence, I'll tell you what I know."

"Where is he?" Colonel de la Chevaux asked.

"Horsey," Hawkeye said, his tone confidential, "I wouldn't want this to get out, but I can tell you, I'm sure. Boris is spending thirty days in the country."

"In the country?" Horsey asked. "Boris gets unnerved when he gets near a Christmas tree. What's he doing in the country?"

"He's in the company of an officer of the law," Hawkeye said, softly. "A very large officer of the law, and when he's not cooking, he's chopping wood."

There was a moment's silence and then a chuckle.

"He's doing thirty days on the country roads, is he?"

---

* Colonel de la Chevaux has for many years served as Supreme Grand Knight Commander of the Peace (sort of Sergeant-at-Arms Plenipotentiary) of the Bayou Perdu Council, Louisiana Consistory, Knights of Columbus. The Bayon Perdu Council is one of the more unusual councils of the K of C, mainly because it holds ten percent of the stock of Chevaux Petroleum Corporation, International. The income from this stock has made possible not only the $2.6-million Council Building in Bayou Perdu, Louisiana, where bar and food service is provided free of charge, twenty-four hours a day, seven days a week to the knights, but the maintenance of annexes of the club house in sixteen locations, from Alaska's north shore to the Kingdom of Hussid and the Sheikhdom of Abzug, wherever their employment with Chevaux Petroleum International has taken Bayou Perdu Council knights. After lengthy negotiations in 1974, presided over by His Eminence John Patrick Mulcahy, titular archbishop of Swengchan, China, chaplain of the council (and formerly chaplain of the 4077th MASH, U.S. Army), agreement was reached with the Framingham Foundation of Cambridge, Massachusetts, giving knights and fellows reciprocal guest privileges. The history of the Bayou Perdu Council was touched upon in M*A*S*H GOES TO NEW ORLEANS (Pocket Books, New York, 1975) for those with an interest in the operation of men's social clubs, and the Washington *Post* (April 11–14, 1975) ran a series of articles charging that the secretary of state not only had accepted an honorary membership in what was described as "a male chauvinist sexist" organization but was known to have participated in full Bayou Perdu Council, K of C, uniform in "drunken revels" in Caracas, Venezuela, and on a drilling platform in the North Sea. The secretary immediately denied any participation in drunken revels but refused comment about his membership, honorary or otherwise.

"You didn't hear that from me," Hawkeye said, quite truthfully.

"Drunk and disorderly?" Horsey inquired. He had had, before and after the discovery under his swamp of "the largest pool of natural gas on the North American continent," enough experience with the law to be fully conversant with the nuances of police-court law enforcement.

"I can swear to you, Horsey, that he wasn't disorderly here."

"I notice you didn't say nothing about drunk."

"And I won't," Hawkeye replied. "But I have it, Horsey, on the very best authority that he was removed from the Framingham Foundation on a stretcher, carried by four of Tranquil Glades' finest."

Horsey chuckled appreciatively.

"Thirty days on the road'll do him a lot of good," Horsey said. "Fresh air, simple food, a little exercise."

"I was thinking precisely the same thing," Hawkeye replied.

"And I can see why he wouldn't want something like that to get out," Horsey said. "I appreciate your telling me this, Hawkeye."

"I didn't tell you anything," Hawkeye said. "Now, can you keep Hassan out of it? I mean, Horsey, the one thing Boris doesn't need is an Arab buddy, right now. The law enforcement officer might misunderstand."

"Gotcha," Horsey said. "I'll think of something to tell Hassan."

"And then you'll have Hassan talk to Esmerelda Hoffenburg and the baroness?"

"No problem," Horsey said. "Boris can do his thirty days without being bothered."

"It's been good to talk to you, Horsey," Hawkeye said. "But I've got to get off the line. There's another call."

"I'll see you in a month," Horsey said. "We'll throw a little 'Welcome Out, Boris' party for him." The line went dead.

It was to ring once more, but not before Hawkeye

had time to relate to Dr. McIntyre and Chief Nurse Flanagan the newest story from the world of grand opera. They were properly appreciative and still chuckling merrily when the phone rang again.

Nurse Flanagan took the call and handed the phone to Trapper John. "It's the fat little kraut," she said, rather skillfully mimicking his manner of speech. "If he's nod tied up or nutting, maybe I could haf a liddle word wit duh doctor?"

"Good afternoon, Mr. Secretary." Trapper John said, briskly, to the telephone. "How are things in international diplomacy?"

"Nod so good, to tell you duh truth," the secretary said. "Be a good boy, Trapper, tell me: You god any idea where is Boris?"

"Boris who?"

"Boris Who Else? How many Borises you know, already?"

"Oh, you mean *that* Boris!"

"I mean *dat* Boris. Where is he? I vant you tell your secretary of state. Uncle Sammy needs to know."

"Might I presume to inquire of you, Mr. Secretary, the reason for your inquiry?"

"You can knock off with duh fancy talk, Trapper, *I'm* the diplomat already."

"Very well," Trapper John replied. "So why do you want to know, Tubby?"

"Vud you believe the French ambassador was just here?"

"I didn't know they were talking to us," Trapper replied.

"Between you and me, I don't know vhy dey are. You vouldn't believe it, if I vas to tell you, vhich I ain't going to, vhat Boris did to their opera."

"Which opera was that?"

"Nod an *opera*," the secretary said. "Vat I mean to say vas what Boris did to dere opera *house*. You know, dat funny-looking building wit' all the dirty statues, around the corner from Harry's New York Bar?"

"I believe I know the place," Trapper John said.

"Vat a mess! Duh ambassador has pictures. He showed me. *Oy vay!* Anyway," the secretary said, "he vas pardoned. The vay I hear it . . . which is from the CIA, so you gotta take it wit' a grain of salt . . . the president's vife moved out and vouldn't move back in until he vas pardoned. Anyvay, dere is a pardon. Duh only little problem is, dere ain't no Boris."

"You don't say?"

"So the French ambassador, vould you believe it, accused me."

"Accused you of what?"

"Of hiding Boris."

"Why would you want to do that?"

"Dat's vat I asked him!"

"And what did he say?"

"He said I vas . . . and me a happily married man . . . trying to make trouble between the president and his vife! Can you believe dat?"

"I believe it," Trapper John said.

"Now duh bottom line," the secretary said. "Can you help me, Trapper?"

"You mean, do I know, and can I tell you, where he is?'

"Dat's right," the secretary said.

"I can tell you this, Tubby," Trapper said, "Waldo Maldemer was just on the phone.'

"Waldo Maldemer? Duh vun vit duh low-slung cheeks? *Dat* Waldo Maldemer?"

"America's most beloved television journalist," Trapper said. "That one."

"Oy vay! And he knows aboud dis?"

"I guess he does," Trapper said. "He led me to believe that he was hot on Boris' tail."

"He didn't happen to mention vere he thought he vas?"

"No," Trapper said. "He just called to check in."

"So I'll call him," the secretary said. "I'll make dat sacrifice."

"That's very noble of you, Mr. Secretary."

"You vouldn't believe, believe me, vat I haf to do in dis job," the secretary said. "Vun more ting, Trapper. If you should happen to bump into Boris somewhere, you'll gif me a call?"

"That I will, Mr. Secretary," Trapper said. He dropped the phone back in its cradle.

"That does it," Hawkeye said. "With the exception of Hot Lips, we've detoured everybody away from here."

"What are you going to do about Hot Lips," John Francis Xavier McIntyre asked, "now that we have been betrayed by this Irish Mata Hari?"

"If worse comes to worse," Hawkeye said, "if it gets to it, I'll bite the bullet and tell her the truth."

"But in the meantime, it's nothing but peace and tranquillity in the deep woods for the big ape, right?" Trapper replied.

"And I'm sure that Hot Lips will be very understanding," Nurse Flanagan said. "So, in a manner of speaking, the crisis is over, right?"

"I know what you're thinking," Trapper John said. "A little less vermouth this time, Flanagan."

Chapter Twelve

At ten minutes past midnight that same night, the radio telephone went off in the deep woods station of the Maine state police.

"Headquarters calling Station Zebra," the radio said. The speaker was located about six inches from the cot on which Boris Alexandrovich Korsky-Rimsakov was sleeping the sound sleep of someone who had just cut a half-cord of wood and then quenched his thirst with a half-gallon of what he thought of as the *vins de pay*. A gallon of the potable had been delivered by Pierre DeBois as a small token of his gratitude to Trooper Harris for his services *vis-à-vis* the arrival of the latest little DeBois. Boris and Steve had meticulously, buddies to the core, split it between them.

Boris, nevertheless, was instantly awake. He grabbed the microphone.

"Go ahead, Headquarters," he said, speaking softly so as not to disturb Steve Harris, who was snoring peacefully on the floor before the fireplace.

"That you, Steve?"

"Steve's not here right now," Boris said. "Can I take a message?"

"Who're you?"

"I'm his cousin George, from Vilewater," Boris lied quickly.

"Well, here's the problem, George," the state police headquarters dispatcher said. "We just got a call from Car Nine-Oh-Seven. He was cruising Interstate Ninety-five up near the potato chip factory. He reports he saw a maritime distress flare being fired over Lost Crystal Lake."

"Over where?"

"The stream they dammed up to make a water supply for the senator's potato chip factory. They call it Lost Crystal Lake."

"So what?" Boris asked reasonably.

"Well, those things are color coded," the dispatcher said. "And the flare . . . actually, Car Nine-Oh-Seven says they're shooting one every three minutes . . . is the one that means, 'Rammed an Iceberg, in Immediate Danger of Sinking.' "

"That's terrible!" Boris replied, compassionately.

"Well," the dispatcher said, "what it probably is is a bunch of kids just horsing around. But they're liable to set a fire with the flares. Can you find Steve and tell him to go have a look?"

"At this time of night? The poor man needs his sleep!"

"He's a Maine state trooper! We never sleep!"

"I got news for you," Boris replied, as Steve let off with a truly magnificent snore. "But I'll tell him. Zebra out."

Boris fixed himself a little eye-opener and then with infinite tenderness woke his friend Steven Harris. Harris, truth to tell, while not exactly a complete stranger to the grape, had had more brewed, fermented, and distilled potables in the last five days than he'd had before in his entire life. That life included the years he had been a Green Beret, and the Green Berets are, whatever their other distinguished accomplishments, best known for their ability to conjure up adequate rations of booze no matter where the exigencies of the service lead them. Harris had tried to drink with Boris, which was beyond his capacity. He was, in fact, still slightly sauced when Boris dragged him erect and woke him. Boris was, as incredible as this might sound, several degrees to the left of absolute sobriety himself.

"I think I'll take a little nap," Steven Harris replied when he finally got Boris' face in focus.

"Duty calls!" Boris said. "Somebody rammed an iceberg in Lost Crystal Lake and is in immediate danger of sinking."

"My God!" Harris said, shaking his head to clear it.

"It came over the radio," Boris announced. "They want you to go over there."

"Certainly," Harris said.

"And I will, of course, go with you," Boris said.

"You're a good guy, Boris," Harris said. In no more then three minutes, the dauntless duo was dressed and ready to face the woods. Arm-in-arm, singing "The Caissons Are Rolling Along," they set out through the deep woods for the maritime disaster on Lost Crystal Lake.

There was, of course, no iceberg on Lost Crystal Lake and no maritime disaster. What had happened was that Wesley St. James had wakened suddenly from his sleep, called, so to speak, by a summons from nature.

As he returned from his mission, terribly relieved to be back in the comforting circle of pup tents and no longer alone out there with God only knew what wild animals, he had shone the beam of his flashlight into the various pup tents, telling himself he was playing a real-life role just like James Arness had played for so many years on "Gunsmoke"; the strong silent figure checking to see that all was right.

Sleep well, my friends, Wesley St. James is watching over you!

The trouble was that everything wasn't what you could call hunky-dory. The pup tent housing Miss LaVerne Schultz held nothing but Miss Schultz's sleeping bag. Wesley St. James got down on his hands and knees and investigated more fully. There was no doubt about it; she was gone.

Still on his hands and knees, Wesley crawled to the next tent, that assigned to Don Rhotten. It had a stake driven into the ground before it, with a small gold star on it.

"Don!" Wesley called. "Don, wake up!"

When there was no response, Wesley tugged gently on Don Rhotten's leg. The result of this was a blood-curdling scream. Don Rhotten exited the tent on the other end from Wesley and scurried, with remarkable speed, up a convenient tree.

"Come down from there, dummy," Wesley hissed. "It's only me!"

"Gee, you got a weird sense of humor, Little Bunny," Don said. "Scaring a guy like that!" He climbed down off the tree. "What the hell do you want, this time of night?"

"LaVerne's not in her tent," Wesley said.

"Shame on you," Don Rhotten said. "Sneaking into her tent!"

"I didn't sneak into it, Don, I shone the flashlight in, and she was gone."

"Well, you know," Don said, "maybe she had to, you know. Girls have to, too, you know."

"I didn't think about that," Wesley said. "You're probably right."

"Of course, I'm right," Don said. "I'm Don Rhotten, you know."

"Well, how about waiting up with me until she comes back?"

"I got a better idea than that," Don said. "Let's wake up the other one and send her looking for LaVerne."

That was a splendid idea, but when Wesley and Don got on their knees to waken Miss Frump, she also was gone.

"My God! They've been carried away by bears!" Wesley said.

"Don't lose control of yourself, Little Bunny," Don Rhotten replied. "You know that girls always go together."

"You really think that's what happened?"

"If you're really scared, Wesley," Don Rhotten said, "wake up Pierre LeGrande. He's the guide. Let him worry about it."

"Good thinking, Don," Wesley said. He crawled over to Pierre LeGrande's pup tent.

"Hey, Frenchie," he called. There was no reply. He called again, and when again there was no response, he felt around inside the tent.

"He's gone, Big Bunny!" he cried.

"You really think he's gone?'

"I know he's gone," Wesley said.

"You were right, Little Bunny," Don Rhotten said. "The bears got him!"

"What are we going to do?" Wesley asked.

"I don't know what you're going to do," Don Rhotten said, with firmness in every syllable, "but I'm going to climb back up the tree."

"I heard somewhere that bears climb trees," Wesley said.

"I'll take my chances," Don Rhotten said, and with that he shinnied back up the tree.

Wesley found an adjacent tree and climbed up that one, too, where for fifteen minutes he clung on for dear life and wondered what he could do. The only consoling thought he could think of was that the bear (*bears,* there must be at least two, and probably three, since three people had been carried off) would probably prefer Don Rhotten who was fatter than he was and would be a more tempting morsel.

But then, ashamed of himself for not thinking of it before and congratulating himself on his foresight, he remembered the flares. The man at the Beverly Hills Safari Outfitters had told him that you never knew when you would need an emergency flare, and Wesley, impressed with the man's concern for his safety, had bought a case of them.

He gathered his courage, slid down the tree, ran to the supply tent, opened the case, filled his pockets with flares, and ran back to the tree.

"You're a brave man, Little Bunny," Don Rhotten said. "I've always said that."

"I know you have, Don," Wesley said. He fired the

first flare. He was a bit (actually, wholly) inexperienced with flares, and the first one he fired went down, not up, setting fire to his pup tent. He consoled himself with the thought that bears would stay away from the fire. Or was it that bears were attracted by fire?

He fired flares every three minutes. They were seen by the night crew at the potato chip factory, of course. But the night foreman decided it was just one more harassment from the clean water kooks, who refused to understand that crudding up one little stream was small enough price to pay for potato chips, particularly when the potato chips were just one more patriotic good work of a senator. He posted guards at the fence line and put in a call to the governor, telling him that the national guard might be needed to protect private property from conservation kooks. Then he called the senator and repeated, word for word, what the governor had said about the senator and his potato chips and what the governor had suggested the senator do with his potato chip factory. The senator cried.

Wesley St. James and Don Rhotten were in the trees, all told, for more than two hours. The supply of flares was exhausted. There was nothing to do but hang on to the trees and await whatever cruel destiny fate had written on their slates.

And then there came the sound of voices, raised in bawdy song, and of feet crashing through the woods. Both Don and Wesley wept tears of relief, but, purely as a precaution, remained in the trees until they saw below them a large state trooper and an equally large civilian (obviously another guide).

"All right," the trooper shouted, "come down out of the trees, kids! The joke is over!"

Wesley St. James slid down the tree. Don Rhotten followed suit. They rushed over to Trooper Harris and Boris and kissed their hands.

"Thank God, we're saved!"

"What are you," Boris inquired, snatching his hand back, "some kind of queer religious nut?"

"Officer," Wesley began. "Sergeant! *Captain!* Our guide and two ladies have been carried off by wild bears!"

"You've got to be kidding," Boris said.

"I'll have a look around," Harris said. He struck Wesley St. James that moment as a reincarnation of James Arness. Tall, large, in charge. "My friend here will stay here and protect you from the bears."

"Oh, thank you!" Don Rhotten said.

"And don't let them shoot off any more flares, Boris," Harris said. He disappeared into the woods.

"Friend, who is that magnificent human being?" Wesley St. James asked.

"I didn't know your kind came out in the woods," Boris replied. "I thought you spent most of your time in closets."

"I'll have you know, sir," Don Rhotten said, "that I am Don Rhotten, America's most beloved young television journalist."

"How do you do?" Boris said. "I'm Boris Alexandrovich Korsky-Rimsakov, the world's greatest opera singer."

"Wise guy!" Wesley St. James snapped.

"What do you mean by that?" Boris snarled.

"Nothing at all," Wesley St. James said quickly. "Nothing at all. It's just that you don't expect to see the world's greatest opera singer in the deep woods."

"You don't expect to see a bald-headed fairy climbing down out of a tree, kissing grown men's hands and trying to tell people he's been chased up there by a bear, either."

"You were telling me about the state trooper," Wesley St. James said.

"Steven Harris," Boris said. "He's my friend."

"I think I'm going to make him a star!" Wesley St. James said.

"What have you guys been drinking?" Boris asked.

"I'm Wesley St. James," Wesley announced. "Known as the Napoleon of Daytime Drama."

"Soap operas, you mean?" Boris asked.

"We don't use that word," Wesley said.

141

"I don't think Steve would be happy in the theater," Boris said.

"The pay is good," Wesley St. James said. "I can see it now: Wesley St. James presents a St. James Production. Steven Harris, Patience Throckbottom Worthington, and Daphne Covington in 'Code of the Deep Woods.'"

"Gee," Don Rhotten said. "That sounds great, Little Bunny!"

"The continuing story of how a courageous grandmother . . . that'll fix that old bitch for holding up Wesley St. James . . . and her family, Sergeant Steven Nobleheart of the Maine Mounted Police, and Carol Nobleheart, his beloved if doomed sister . . . face the stark life with all its pathos, pain, and tragedy, in the deep woods."

"Not a chance," Boris replied. (He was, after all, not entirely inexperienced in dealing with theatrical producers. He had not become the world's highest-paid opera singer because the producers had liked the sound of his voice, as he often said. It wasn't that Boris disliked producers . . . he felt, as a group, that they were every bit as nice as people who poison Halloween candy and just as valuable to society as congressmen . . . but rather that they tested his mettle. He had as much trouble dealing with producers as he did getting the corks out of champagne bottles: they always came out in the end, of course. The only thing that changed was the sound of the gas escaping.)

"What do you mean, 'not a chance'?" Wesley St. James asked. This was not the response he was used to getting when he announced that he was going to make someone a star.

"My client considers your opening offer, for someone of his talents and desirability in the marketplace, insulting. We're just going to have to go to . . . what did you say your network was?"

"ABS," Don Rhotten said.

"CBS," Boris said. "Their offer was a lot better."

"I didn't make an offer," Wesley St. James said.

"Well, there you are," Boris said. "Now why don't you fold up your tent, little man, so you can steal away when my client returns?'

"Five hundred dollars a week," Wesley St. James said.

"Or maybe NBC," Boris said, thoughtfully. "They know the value of talent when they see it."

"Seven-fifty," Wesley St. James said.

"Tell you what I'll do, little man with funny hair," Boris said. "To show you that my heart's in the right place, we'll split the difference. Call it a thousand a week and certain perks . . . you know what perks are . . . and you've got a deal."

"What kind of perks?" Wesley St. James asked.

"I'll send you a list," Boris said. "Yes or no? I don't have all night to stand around in the middle of the woods arguing with you."

"You've got yourself a deal," Wesley St. James said.

"Ordinarily," Boris said, "I would shake hands. But under these circumstances, I think I'd rather not."

"How soon can your client start to work?"

"Just as soon as your check for a month's advance salary clears," Boris said. "You understand, of course, that he is to be paid in advance?"

"I don't have a checkbook."

"Cash will do," Boris said. "Say a thousand right now, for earnest money."

As Wesley St. James searched for his wallet, found it, and started to unzip it, there came the sound of several animate objects marching through the woods.

"My God!" Don Rhotten said, heading back for his tree. "Just at the moment when Wesley St. James was to create another star, we're all going to be eaten by bears."

"Shut up, Don," Wesley St. James said. The fear of bears was behind him. He had *that* feeling; he knew he was on the threshold of the greatest triumph of his daytime drama career.

It wasn't a herd of bears. It was Trooper Steven Harris

of the Maine state police. He held Miss LaVerne Schultz's arm in his left hand, Miss Louella Frump's arm in his right hand. Pierre LeGrande, a/k/a Angelo Napolitano, trudged along behind them, head bent, looking somewhat chagrined.

"I have good news," Harris said. "Your friends have not been eaten by bears."

"Say, Pierre," Don Rhotten asked, "what happened to your pants?" He paused and then went on. "And for that matter, LaVerne, what happened to yours?"

"That's the bad news," Trooper Harris said. "I'm afraid I must tell you that Angelo has broken Rule Three of the code of the deep woods."

"What's that?"

"Guides are not supposed to fool around with guidees," Harris said.

"I've got good news for you, too," Boris said.

"What's that?" Harris asked.

"You have just become a television star at one-thousand dollars a week," Boris said. "Plus perks."

"Not now, Boris," Steven Harris said. "Be a good guy and cool the imagination until I get these four kooks out of the woods, will you?"

"Give him the long green, little man," Boris ordered.

Wesley St. James walked up to Trooper Harris and handed him one-thousand dollars.

"What's this for?"

"I just told you," Boris said. "You have just become a star."

The scene shifts, as they say in the trade, to glamorous Hollywood, California, specifically to the Wesley St. James Productions studios and to the interior of Miss Patience Throckbottom Worthington's trailer.

Miss Worthington is dressed for her role as Sister Piety on the daytime drama "Guiding Torch." Such is her inimitable talent for creating an image that she really looks like a nun, even though she is sitting, a foot-long cigarette holder in her mouth, a martini glass in her hand, and (her vestments hiked rather high) displaying a good deal of leg, on a barstool in her trailer.

Wesley St. James is dressed as he was dressed in the deep woods of Maine—that is to say, in a genuine safari jacket, an Australian bush hat, riding breeches, and glistening boots. He believes this gives him a certain aura of machismo.

Miss Worthington takes the cigarette holder from her mouth, looks at Wesley St. James with absolute loathing, and speaks.

"If you really think that Patience T. Worthington is going to go on bleeping location in the bleeping woods to play some bleeping backwoods earth mother, you've got another bleeping think coming, you bleeping little blap."

"Miss Worthington," Wesley St. James said, "you asked me to come up with a vehicle in which the many facets of your extraordinary talent could be fully utilized," Wesley St. James said.

"Patience T. Worthington, playing with two bleeping unknowns? I don't even know what these two blaps you've come up with bleeping well look like."

"I have glossy photographs right here, Miss Worthington," Wesley St. James said. He handed her two photographs. One was an 8 x 10 glossy photograph of Zelda Spinopolous, taken some years before when she was a student at Ingrid Posnofski's Studio of the Dance in Cicero, Illinois. It showed her, her blond hair in pigtails, wearing a sailor suit, performing a tap dance.

"That's Daphne Covington," Wesley St. James said.

Miss Worthington studied the photograph carefully, both because she was on her fifth martini and things were a little blurry and because long experience had taught her to watch out for young broads who were liable to steal your scene. In her professional judgment, Daphne Covington couldn't possibly pose such a threat.

"O.K.," she said. "She looks like something that wouldn't have the bleeping sense to get her tail out of the bleeping forest."

145

The second photograph was a Polaroid color shot taken just two days before in the woods by Don Rhotten. (He had taken a Polaroid camera with him into the woods, although he hadn't had photographs exactly like this in mind; he had really been thinking of taking some "nature" shots of the ladies, au naturel.)

This showed Trooper Steven J. Harris, Mr. Wesley St. James, and Boris Alexandrovich Korsky-Rimsakov. Trooper Harris was smiling nervously at the camera. Wesley St. James, who had drawn himself up to his full five-feet-four, was smiling at Trooper Harris. Boris was unaware he was in the picture at all. He was in the act of holding up the advance cash payment Mr. St. James had given to Trooper Harris to make sure the bills had been printed by the United States government.

"Well, there's your star," Wesley St. James said.

"Not bad," Miss Worthington said.

"A true child of the woods," Wesley St. James said. "All man and a yard wide."

"So it would appear."

"The kind of face that will really reach out and grab the hearts of women," Wesley St. James said, "and let them simultaneously hate and love you as the source of his inspiration and strength."

"You know," Miss Worthington said, almost fondly, "you little blap, I have to hand it to you. You have finally come up with a man to play against me with whom, I sense in my bones, I will have a great rapport, a mingling of the souls. We will make great television, and some other things, together."

"I thought you would approve."

"I have only two questions, Wesley," she said. "What's he doing with the money, and who's the ugly cop you're looking at like a lovesick calf?"

Chapter Thirteen

Thirty-eight percent of the petroleum supplies of France, as has been previously stated, originate beneath the sands of the kingdom of Hussid. For that reason, the French government is understandably willing, even eager, to "cooperate" with representatives of that Islamic nation whenever they have a small request to make.

As the president of the republic stated to his cabinet, "Whatever Hussid wants, fellas, Hussid gets."

It wasn't only the oil that placed Hussid high in French esteem and made them unusually sensitive to Hussid's feelings. Air Hussid, wholly owned by the government of Hussid, which is to say the Royal Family, was one of the few customers France had for its famous, supersonic jet transport, *Le Discorde*. *Le Discorde* was truly a magnificent flying machine that could fly faster and farther than any other airliner in commercial service. There was only one small problem with it. It carried only sixty-eight passengers in the "tourist" configuration and forty-four in the first-class configuration. (First-class passengers were not required to ride with their knees under their chins.) When seat space was computed against air speed and hourly operating costs, airline cost accountants had come up with what is known as the "seat-mile figure." This is how much it cost one passenger to go one mile. In the belief that there really wasn't much of a market for air transport, even supersonically, or even considering inflight snacks catered by Maxim's at the rate of $0.35 per seat air mile (or $1,697.50 one way between New York and Paris, as opposed to a first-class price of

$501.10 on an old-fashioned Boeing 747), the world's airlines had been somewhat reluctant to buy *Le Discorde.*

This was denounced by the French government as one more proof of CIA interference in international affairs, but to no avail. The only airline that purchased *Le Discorde* (except of course, Air Hussid) was Air France. Air France, like Aero-Industrie Française, which manufactured *Le Discorde,* is government owned, and since it is spending the taxpayers' money, is not forced to consider such archaic notions as profit and loss.

Air Hussid bought six *Le Discorde* aircraft as a gesture of Franco-Hussid friendship. One of them was reserved for the personal use of His Islamic Majesty the King, and one each was assigned to His Islamic Majesty's ambassadors to France, the United States, and Japan. One *Le Discorde* was converted to cargo usage and plied regularly between Paris and El Lio, Hussid's capital, carrying freshly baked French bread, croissants, snails, caviar, and other delicacies. The sixth plane was given to Sheikh Abdullah ben Abzug, reigning monarch of the shiekhdom of Abzug, in keeping with the old Arabic customs of hospitality.

"What the hell is that?" asked the sheikh of the king, when he saw the somewhat odd-looking craft at El Lio International Airport.

"It's yours," replied the king. "I have half a dozen."

Few Americans, not including the secretary of state, understood the relationship between the governments of France and Hussid. One of those who understood it rather well was Colonel Jean-Pierre de la Chevaux, president and chief executive officer of the Chevaux Petroleum Corporation, International, who was a close friend of both the heir apparent to the throne of Hussid, His Royal Highness Prince Hassan, and His Islamic Majesty, Sheikh Abdullah ben Abzug.

The Royal Hussid–Bayou Perdu Oil Corporation, a joint venture of His Islamic Majesty and the Chevaux Petroleum Corporation, held the monopoly on Abzugian oil. As a token of respect, His Majesty had ennobled

Colonel de la Chevaux as Sheikh Seroh Ecaf, and his Islamic Majesty, in turn, had been admitted to membership in the Bayou Perdu Council, K of C, and subsequently appointed Grand Knight Commander of the Ballet, His Majesty having shown a deep interest in the Bayou Perdu Council's marching baton twirlers.

Shortly after talking to Dr. Pierce on the telephone, Colonel de la Chevaux departed Bayou Perdu International Airport aboard Chevaux Petroleum's Learjet Number Two for Paris. His trip had a double purpose. For one thing, he wanted to see with his own eyes the damage that Boris had caused backstage at the Paris Opéra during his unsuccessful search for the property master, and secondly, he knew that His Royal Highness Prince Hassan would be upset over his missing buddy, and he suspected that it would be far better to gently, and personally, tell Hassan that Boris was doing thirty days on the Spruce Harbor County road gang as penance for drunk-and-disorderly conduct than it would be to try to pass on this information over the telephone, especially since it was common knowledge that Hassan's phone had been tapped by the French Secret Service, or Deuxieme Bureau.

Colonel de la Chevaux was somewhat surprised to see all the *Le Discorde* aircraft lined up at Paris' Orly Field. Both of the *Le Discorde*s that Air France owned, of course (the wooden mockup and the one that actually flew), were there, parked so as to impress the tourists.

But there also were three other *Le Discorde*s sitting there. Two bore the insignia of Air Hussid (a spouting oil well, framed with dollar signs), but neither of them was the *Le Discorde* converted to cargo service. The third *Le Discorde* bore the insignia of Air Abzug (golden wings with Arabic letters spelling out "THIS IS MINE, SHEIKH ABDULLAH") on nose, wings, and vertical stabilizer.

Immediately upon disembarking from his Learjet, Colonel de la Chevaux got on the telephone. The Royal Hussid Embassy (located in the Hotel Continental) replied that His Royal Highness Prince Hassan was off on the kingdom's diplomatic business and there was no indication of when he might return.

The embassy of the shiekhdom of Abzug denied unequivocally that His Majesty was in France. That meant only one thing. Horsey trotted through Orly Field's terminal building, jumped into a cab, and gave an address on a side street off the Champs Elysées.

He knew he had guessed right when he saw the fleets of cars lining the street and the two dozen robed bodyguards slouching around amusing themselves by pointing their silver-plated submachine guns at the gendarmes and passersby.

Horsey paid off the cab, jumped out, and started to run across the street.

There was a burst of submachine-gun fire at his feet. He stopped in his tracks. He glowered at the robed Arabs running toward him.

"What's the matter with you clowns?" he said, in fluent Arabic. "Don't you recognize Ol' Horsey?"*

"May Allah forgive us!" one six-foot-three Nubian bodyguard said, falling to his knees and banging his head three times on the sidewalk.

"It is His Most Gracious Excellency, Sheikh Seroh Ecaf," another bodyguard said. "And we nearly killed him! Forgive us, oh merciful one!"

"I've told you guys and told you guys," Horsey said, a little annoyed, "first you look and *then* you shoot!"

"We humbly beg your pardon, oh noble sheikh!" the two said, in unison.

"Just watch it," Horsey said. "It's just lucky for you that you can't hit your own. . . ." He stopped. "Stop

---

* Colonel de la Chevaux, who has something of a flair for languages, has "picked up" what he terms the "lingo" of the lands in which he has "sunk holes." He is thus able to conduct business negotiations with high-ranking officials of every country in which Chevaux Petroleum has "sunk holes" except for Nigeria. Nigeria was formerly a British colony, and most of its senior officers speak Oxfordian English. When transacting business in Nigeria, Colonel de la Chevaux, to his great embarrassment, is forced to employ an interpreter.

banging your foreheads on the sidewalk!" he said. "Enough, already!"

He continued across the street, past other bodyguards who snapped to attention as he passed, and passed through the well-guarded doors of the place where he had known Prince Hassan and the sheikh would be. The sign over the door read "CRAZY HORSE SALOON."

His Royal Highness Prince Hassan, as a devout follower of the Prophet, was a total teetotaler. When Horsey entered the darkened room, His Highness was weeping softly into his Gatorade, barely able to see Miss Susie-Q and her Counterrotating Mammary Protuberances on the stage. His Majesty Sheikh Abdullah was also, of course, a devout follower of the Prophet, and while he scrupulously followed the Prophet's admonition to abjure the fermented grape, he also noticed that the Prophet had nothing whatever to say about the fermented plum, and he was therefore weeping into a large glass of slivovitz, to which potable he had been introduced by the missing Boris Alexandrovich Korsky-Rimsakov.

"Ah, Horsey," the sheikh said, getting to his feet, wrapping Horsey in his arms, and kissing him wetly on each cheek. "You have come, beloved friend, to share our sorrow."

"If I've told you once, Abdullah, I've told you fifty times. I don't like to be kissed! What if somebody saw me letting you do that!"

"Have you heard anything, Horsey?" Prince Hassan asked.

"As a matter of fact, I have," Horsey said.

"Is El Noil Sniol all right?" Abdullah asked.

"As well as can be expected under the circumstances," Horsey replied. He waved his hand at a waiter, and a bottle of Old White Stagg Blended Kentucky Bourbon was brought to the table.

"Don't keep us waiting," Hassan said.

"The thing is, I promised I wouldn't tell," Horsey said.

"Give us a hint," Hassan said.

"Boris is doing thirty days on the county road in Maine," Horsey said, "for drunk and disorderly."

"But he is always drunk and disorderly," Sheikh Abdullah replied.

"In Maine, it is against the customs," Horsey explained. "He'll be out in less than a month, and I think, under the circumstances, that we should not let him know we know what has happened to him."

"You mean to say that he has been *arrested?*" Sheikh Abdullah said.

"Arrested and sentenced," Horsey said. "Sometimes known as bagged and jugged."

"May I tell Esmerelda and the baroness?" Hassan asked. "They were quite distraught."

"I wish you wouldn't," Horsey said. "Let's just keep it between us. O.K.?"

"Whatever you say," Hassan said. "I'm just relieved that he is alive."

Sheikh Abdullah rose to his feet and walked in the direction of the men's room. But he stopped at a pay telephone. One of his bodyguards, after a word of command, put a coin in the slot and then dialed the number for him. He spoke briefly on the telephone and then handed the headset to the guard, who hung it up for him.

Then he returned to the table.

"I deeply regret that I must take my leave," he said. "Pressing affairs of state."

"Oh, have another snort, Abdullah," Horsey said. "The broad can wait a little."

"The honor of Abzug is at stake," Sheikh Abdullah said.

"You guys take the whole business much too seriously," Horsey said.

Sheikh Abdullah didn't reply. He made a regal gesture of farewell, turned around, and marched out of the Crazy Horse Saloon. His bodyguard, waiting on the sidewalk, snapped to attention. He stepped into the back of his Rolls-Royce. Sirens began to scream. Preceded by Land-

Rovers jammed full of bodyguards, the Rolls-Royce rolled down Rue Pierre Charron, turned left on the Champs Elysées, and, gathering speed, drove down it to the Place de la Concorde.

As they passed through the Place de la Concorde, the sheikh looked to his left, at the American embassy, and nodded his approval when he saw another Rolls, like his flying the flag of the sheikhdom of Abzug, roll up before the gates.

His convoy crossed the Seine and headed for Orly Field. As he had ordered, the royal *Le Discorde* was ready for him. Ninety seconds after he boarded the plane, Orly Control cleared Abzug Air Force One for immediate takeoff.

By the time his *Le Discorde* reached altitude and left French airspace, the high-speed teletypewriter in the bowels of the State Department in Washington, D.C., was already chattering out its somewhat disturbing message.

FROM U.S. EMBASSY, PARIS
TO SECRETARY OF STATE, WASHINGTON, D.C.
OPERATIONAL URGENT PRIORITY
TOP SECRET—FOR EYES OF DEPUTY SECRETARIES OF STATE AND UP ONLY

1. AT 10:15 ZULU TIME THIS DATE THE AMBASSADOR OF THE SHEIKHDOM OF ABZUG REQUESTED AN AUDIENCE WITH THE U.S. AMBASSADOR TO FRANCE.
2. AT 10:20 HOURS ZULU THIS DATE THE AMBASSADOR OF THE SHEIKHDOM OF ABZUG PRESENTED HIS CREDENTIALS TO THE U.S. AMBASSADOR TO FRANCE AT THE U.S. EMBASSY.
3. AT 10:21 HOURS ZULU THIS DATE, THE AMBASSADOR OF THE SHEIKHDOM OF ABZUG PRESENTED THE FOLLOWING NOTE TO THE U.S. AMBASSADOR FOR TRANSMISSION TO THE SECRETARY OF STATE. QUOTE: "IT HAS COME TO THE ATTENTION OF HIS MOST

MERCIFUL MAJESTY SHEIKH ABDULLAH BEN ABZUG,
MAY HIS TRIBE INCREASE, MAY HIS OLIVE TREES AND
HERDS OF SHEEP BE FRUITFUL, MAY HIS ENEMIES
DEVELOP BOILS ON THEIR REPRODUCTIVE ORGANS,
THAT HIS EXCELLENCY SHEIKH EL NOIL SNIOL, AM-
BASSADOR EXTRAORDINARY AND PLENIPOTENTIARY
OF HIS MOST ISLAMIC MAJESTY TO THE WORLD AND
IN POSSESSION OF ABZUGIAN DIPLOMATIC PASSPORT
NUMBER SIX, HAS BEEN ARRESTED IN MAINE, U.S.A.,
AND IS CURRENTLY IMPRISONED THERE. THE ARREST
OF A DIPLOMATIC REPRESENTATIVE OF HIS MOST
ISLAMIC MAJESTY IS A BLATANT, GROSS VIOLATION
OF INTERNATIONAL LAW AND CUSTOM AND AN IN-
TOLERABLE AFFRONT TO THE DIGNITY OF HIS ISLAMIC
MAJESTY. THEREFORE, UNLESS THE SAID SHEIKH EL
NOIL SNIOL THE MAGNIFICENT IS INSTANTLY, IM-
MEDIATELY, FORTHWITH, AND WITH PROFUSE APOLO-
GIES RELEASED FROM IMPRISONMENT, THE GOVERN-
MENT OF HIS MAJESTY SHEIKH ABDULLAH BEN
ABZUG, MAY HIS TRIBE INCREASE, ETC., ETC., WILL
CONSIDER THAT A STATE OF WAR EXISTS BETWEEN
THE UNITED STATES OF AMERICA AND THE ISLAMIC
SHEIKHDOM OF ABZUG. IN THE BELIEF, HOWEVER,
THAT THE U.S. SECRETARY OF STATE WILL RECOG-
NIZE THAT AN INJUSTICE OF THE GREATEST MAGNI-
TUDE HAS TAKEN PLACE AND INSTANTLY IF NOT
SOONER ARRANGE FOR THE RELEASE OF SHEIKH EL
NOIL SNIOL THE MAGNIFICENT, FROM DURANCE VILE,
HIS MOST GRACIOUS MAJESTY SHEIKH ABDULLAH HAS
MOST GRACIOUSLY DEPARTED FOR THE UNITED
STATES TO PERSONALLY ACCEPT THE PROFOUND AND
HUMBLE APOLOGIES OF THE SECRETARY OF STATE,
AFTER WHICH HIS ISLAMIC MAJESTY WILL GRA-
CIOUSLY ACCEPT THE HOSPITALITY OF THE SECRE-
TARY OF STATE AT THAT LITTLE PLACE ON Q STREET
NORTHWEST CALLED, HIS MAJESTY THINKS, THE
HOTSY-TOTSY TOPLESS TOREADOR. I HAVE THE HONOR
TO BE YOUR MOST OBEDIENT AND HUMBLE SERVANT,
SHEIKH OMAR EL KASZAM, AMBASSADOR OF THE

SHEIKHDOM OF HIS MOST ISLAMIC MAJESTY SHEIKH ABDULLAH BEN ABZUG, MAY HIS TRIBE INCREASE, ETC., ETC.

4. AT 10:23 HOURS ZULU TIME THIS DATE, THE ABZUGIAN AMBASSADOR, AFTER EXPRESSING THE MOST INSULTING COMMENTS THIS CAREER DIPLO-MAT HAS EVER HEARD ON THE WAY THE U.S. DIPLO-MATIC SERVICE IS CONDUCTED, DEPARTED THE U.S. EMBASSY.

FOR THE AMBASSADOR:
ISAAC S. RONALD
DEPUTY ASSISTANT CHIEF,
POLITICO-MILITARY AFFAIRS

The message was immediately brought to the secre-tary's attention, of course. Soon the pathetic cry *"Oy vay iz mir!"* could be heard emitting from the executive staff sauna bath on the sixth floor, whence the secretary had gone following an appearance on Capitol Hill before the Senate Foreign Relations Subcommittee, whose chair-man was either unwilling or unable to understand that it would not be a good thing, diplomacy-wise, to serve hog jowls and grits to the emperor of Japan on his for-mal visit, no matter how popular that was back in the the senator's home town.

Wrapped modestly in a towel and looking, as he strode purposefully down the highly polished marble corridors of the palace presented to our hard-working diplomats by an adoring populace, not unlike a plump Roman solon of the third century B.C., the secretary went to his office. The sight of him waddling along in his bare feet rather shocked the eighth and ninth grades of Saint Bona-venture's Junior High School, of Bogota, New Jersey. who were touring the State Department, even though they had been forewarned that a good deal of peculiar things happened around the State Department.

The secretary went behind his desk and instructed

155

his secretary to get the governor of Maine on the line, instantly.

"Governor, this is the secretary of state," he said when the phone buzzed. "What do you mean, how do you know that? Lissen, didn't my secretary tell you I was? Would a nice shiksa girl like that lie to you?" Pause. "Listen, Governor, Uncle Sammy needs a little favor."

The governor, truth to tell, was not overly awed by our servants of the people in our nation's capital. The kindest word he had used to describe them in his last speech was "scalawags." It was fortunate, therefore, that the secretary of state had evoked the image of Uncle Sam. If he had asked for a favor, either personally or in his office as secretary of state, the odds are that the governor would have given him the same suggestion, vis-à-vis his favor, as he had offered the night foreman of the potato chip factory vis-à-vis the factory.

But the governor could not, as a patriotic man, refuse a favor asked in the name of Uncle Sam, who was after all a Maine man.*

"What's the favor?" he asked, with what cannot truthfully be described as great enthusiasm.

"It seems you've got some Abzugian in the slammer up there," the secretary of state said.

"What's an Abzugian?"

"It's like an Arab, but worse," the secretary replied.

"You say he's in the slammer? What did he do?"

"You're the governor," the secretary replied. "You should know."

"I'm the governor, not the warden of the state prison," the governor replied. "But go on. I always like a little joke."

"I don't know what he did," the secretary confessed. "All I know is that unless he gets a pardon, we're in trouble, Governor."

"What do you mean, *we're* in trouble?" the governor inquired.

---

* This is the subject of some historical controversy; not, however, in Maine.

"It means war," the secretary said. "We just got an ultimatum."

"From some country I never heard of?"

"Trust me. I know it exists," the secretary said. "The . . . whatchamacallit, the head man, the *shiekh,* is a personal friend of mine."

"With friends like yours, Mr. Secretary, this country doesn't need any enemies," the governor said.

"What do you want me to do, Governor, get down on my hands and knees and beg?"

"Why not?"

"So I'm on my hands and knees," the secretary replied. (This was, in fact, what is known as a little diplomatic white lie. He feared that if he actually got on his hands and knees, the towel would fall off. He didn't like to think what his secretary would think if she should come into his office and see him there, on his knees, in his birthday suit.)

"O.K.," the governor said. "What's his name? I'll pardon him on condition that you get him out of Maine and keep him out."

"His name is El Noil Sniol the Magnificent," the secretary said.

"You're kidding," the governor said.

"I am not kidding," the secretary said in righteous indignation. "That's what it says on the teletype, and I'm looking at it."

"What do I do with him when I pardon him? Just kick him outside the prison gate?"

"No!" the secretary said. "Hang on to him. Just as soon as I get off the phone, I'm on my way to come get him."

"What do you want him for?"

"He's really the Abzugian Ambassador Extraordinary and Plenipotentiary," the secretary said.

"Then how did he wind up in my jail?"

"I wish I knew," the secretary said. "Look, it's been nice talking to you, Governor, but my towel just slipped."

"I beg your pardon?"

"My towel just came off," the secretary replied. There then came a female scream, "You dirty old man!", a female voice cried, "Shame on you!", and at that point the connection was broken.

Chapter Fourteen

Zelda Spinopolous entered the world of show business, if not kicking and screaming, then with something less than the breathless enthusiasm of most young women in similar circumstances.

She had heard, of course, of screen tests and of their importance in the selection of actresses for roles of absolutely minimal importance, not to mention instant stardom, and she prepared carefully for hers. The screen test was conducted in ABS Television's Chicago studios. She entered the building a rather startlingly good-looking young female, in the first blush of womanhood. She spent a full hour preparing herself in the dressing room provided for her and blessing the memory of her childhood chum Oscar Whaley, who had taught her a theatrical trick, what is known in show business as a "schtick," which he felt she could put to good use.

Finally she was led before the cameras, having first sent out word that she was so nervous she couldn't stand the thought of having anyone, especially her mother, on her set. Mrs. Gustaphalous Spinopolous (the crew having had previous experience with stage mothers) was gotten off the set by the simple device of calling her to the telephone for a little chat with a vice-president of ABS, who conducted a lengthy interview with the mother of the star, allegedly for release to what he termed the "printed media."

The wholesome, attractive, indeed even sexy young woman who had come to the studios from the biology laboratories of the University of Chicago was gone. The blond hair was now parted neatly in the middle, brushed tight against the skull, and caught up in a sort of scraggly bun in the back. The blue eyes were now visible only through thick granny glasses perched crookedly on her nose. A good deal of mascara had been applied, but below the eye, so that it gave the appearance that Miss Spinopolous was approaching death's dark door. Additional mascara had been applied over two of her normally pearly white teeth, giving the appearance that those teeth were missing. Her figure, which had been previously covered by a rather close-fitting pair of blue jeans and a crisp white blouse, against which her mammary development had pushed attractively if modestly, was now wholly concealed within an ill-fitting cotton dress she had had the foresight to pick up at the Salvation Army.

The Wesley St. James Productions crew, which had been flown in from the West Coast (en route to Maine) to make the test, was not disturbed by the frightening apparition that limped onto the sound stage. They simply, and with good reason, concluded that there had been a slight administrative mixup, and that the testee was being tested for one of the St. James Games. St. James Games, in the interests of what was known as "audience identification," conducted a year-round search for the grotesque, ludicrous, and pathetic. In their judgment, this freaky broad was sure to win a place on a St. James game, most likely "Money for Your Misery."

"All right, honey," the director said. "When I call 'roll e'm,' I want you to look right at the camera and read what's written on the thing over the camera. It's called the idiot board, but don't you mind that."

"Right," Zelda replied.

"Roll 'em," the director replied.

Zelda, her mouth hanging slackly open, her shoulders hunched forward, peered intently at the idiot board (this was no show business schtick; she could hardly see the device through her thick granny glasses) and proceeded to read it, as slowly as she could, mispronouncing as many words as she thought she could get away with. When she had finished reading the few lines ("Hello there, I'm Daphne Covington, and I'm going to be visiting you every weekday on the new Wesley St. James Production, "The Code of the Deep Woods." in which I play the role of Carol Nobleheart. Please watch!") she removed the granny glasses and did her schtick, learned at the age of thirteen from good old Oscar Whaley. First her eyes crossed, both pointing at her nose. Then the left eye slowly began to revolve. It was enough to turn the stomach of a strong man.

"Cut!" the director called, enthusiastically. "Thank you very much, Miss Spinopolous. That was fine. I'm sure you'll be hearing from St. James Games very shortly." He turned to his chief engineer. "Rewind the tape," he ordered, "and get ready for transmisson to New York. The big shots are waiting for it."

Zelda Spinopolous literally skipped off the sound stage. She went to the dressing room smiling happily to herself. This television nonsense was a dead issue. She would soon be left alone with her microscope and her protozoa cultures. No one in his right mind would put someone like that on the tube.

While it is true that when the tape was run in the executive projection room there were some murmurs of disapproval, and even some groans when she rolled her left eye, there never was any question of nipping the television career of Miss Daphne Covington in the bud. After all, how many actresses who could roll their left eye were the only daughters of Chef Pierre, whose advertising budget represented somewhere between 18 and 23 percent of ABS' advertising revenue?

"We'll shoot her through a soft-focus lens . . ." one ABS biggie said.

"Why don't we just shoot her?" another biggie asked. "That would seem to be the kindest thing to do."

"Ernie, you're not thinking like a team player," the vice-president for advertising said, gently. "Rethink that."

161

"And we'll get somebody to dub her voice," the first biggie said.

"Take a telegram," the vice-president for advertising said to his secretary. "Miss Daphne Covington, Chicago. All of us here at ABS were deeply affected when we viewed your test. Welcome, welcome to the happy television family of ABS."

Miss Covington was not the only reluctant thespian. Trooper Steven Harris of the Maine state police had to have a little chat with the governor before he put his signature on the contract.

The governor, as it happened, was an old friend of Dr. Benjamin Franklin Pierce, chief of surgery of the Spruce Harbor Medical Center. He had just taken a call from the secretary of state when his secretary informed him that Dr. Pierce was on the line.

"O.K., Hawkeye," the governor said, grabbing the phone, "score one for the chancre mechanic. You really had me fooled."

"Fooled about what, Your Most Bureaucratic Majesty?" Hawkeye replied. "I just called to ask for a favor."

"That wasn't you on the phone just now?"

"Boy scout's honor," Hawkeye said. "I just this minute came into the office."

"It sounded like something you'd think up," the governor said. "Would you believe that the secretary of state was just on the phone?"

"I'd believe anything of the secretary of state," Hawkeye said. "You want to tell me about it?"

"No," the governor said. "I can't stand that cackling laugh of yours. What's on your mind, pecker checker?"

"I want you to fire one of your state troopers," Hawkeye said.

"No," the governor said immediately. "What we hire them for is to keep maniacs like you off the highway. What did he get you for?"

"As a matter of fact, he's a friend of mine," Hawkeye said. "This is really in his best interests."

"I really hate to ask this, but do you want to tell me what the problem is?"

"Well, Ludwell, it's like this . . ." Hawkeye began.

"I've asked you not to call me that, Hawkeye," the governor said.

"I won't ever again, if you promise to fire the cop," Hawkeye said.

"It's that important to you, is it?" asked the governor, who loathed his first name quite as much as Hawkeye loved it.

"Let me tell you the situation," Hawkeye said. He then proceeded to tell the governor most of the details of the Wesley St. James Productions offer of $1,000 a week for Steve Harris' services as a television thespian. He left out, of course, any reference to Boris Alexandrovich Korsky-Rimsakov. He merely related that Mr. St. James had become very impressed with Trooper Harris when Harris had come to his aid in the deep woods and that, "in the opinion of a friend of mine with some experience with theatrical contracts," the contract, "as amended by my friend," was written so that Harris could earn enough money to pursue his medical education even if not a single foot of film was shot.

The only little problem was that Harris refused to sign the contract. The loggers in the deep woods and their families needed him, he said, and besides, he had sort of enlisted in the state police and felt that turning his uniform in would be letting the side down. The obvious solution was to fire him.

"You pose quite an ethical problem, Hawkeye," the governor said, thoughtfully. "On one hand, I am deeply sympathetic to your position. We certainly need . . . especially when we consider people like you . . . medical doctors with a deep devotion to people, and I realize that about the best possible way to get the money to pay for their education is from those expletive deleted television people. On the other hand, however, I have an obligation to the rest of the state troopers. Think what having a boob-tube idiot dressed in one of their uniforms is going to do to their morale. They'll be ashamed to be seen on the highways."

"Ludwell, I hate to press you," Hawkeye said. "I see your problem, Ludwell, but, Ludwell, under these circumstances, I feel, Ludwell . . ."

"You win," the governor said. "I'll call him in right now."

"Thank you, Your Most Bureaucratic Majesty," Hawkeye said. "I knew I could count on you in a pinch."

"Are you going to see Trapper John anytime soon?" the governor asked.

"In just a couple of minutes," Hawkeye replied. "We're going to jerk a gall bladder."

"Tell him," the governor said, "to go [scatological reference deleted]."

"That's a physiological impossibility," Hawkeye replied. "May I inquire as to the reason for your displeasure with Dr. McIntyre?"

"He sent the results of my Wasserman test to my home."

"Negative, I trust?" Hawkeye asked.

"I didn't take a Wasserman test," the governor replied.

"Then there must be some mistake."

"You want to try to explain that to my wife, Hawkeye?" the governor replied. "I've tried."

"No problem at all," Hawkeye said. "If you'll spell her first name for me, I'll see that you have the report . . . positive . . . of her Wasserman in the morning mail. You're a politician, you should be able to take it from there."

"God," the governor said, with awe, respect, and sincerity in every quivering syllable, "you really are a devious, Machiavellian scoundrel, Hawkeye. I'm glad you didn't go into politics. That's spelled M,Y,R,T,L,E."

"Nice to talk to you, Your Bureaucratic Majesty," Hawkeye said. "Knowing that people like you are in high elective office almost . . . not quite, but almost . . . restores my faith in our political system."

The governor broke the connection with his finger and got his secretary on the line.

"Call the head of the state police and tell him to have a Trooper Steven J. Harris report to me immediately," he said. "And then call the warden and ask him what kind of a prison he's running if he can't find one lousy Abzugian ambassador in his slammer."

"He called while you were speaking with Dr. Pierce, Governor," his secretary reported. "He says he's got three Lebanese, four Chinese, one South African, two Turks, and a Bohemian. But no Abzugian."

"Tell him to keep looking!" the governor snapped and hung up.

Three hours later, as the governor was rehearsing, in the governor's private wash room mirror, the look of righteous indignation he was going to give his wife at the breakfast table, the telephone rang.

"It's about time you called," he snapped. "You have found the Abzugian, I hope?"

"It's me, Governor," his secretary replied. "There has been no word from the warden."

"I told you not to put any other calls through," the governor said. "I have enough trouble with Washington because of that potato chip senator of ours. I don't want them laughing at me because I can't find their Abzugian for them."

"This isn't a call, Governor," she said. "Trooper Harris is here, with orders to report to you."

"Send him in."

The governor was a persuasive man, with long experience in getting people to change their minds when their minds were firmly made up. It took him two-and-a-half hours before he finally got Steven J. Harris to admit that his leave of absence from the state police was in the best interests of medicine, the state of Maine (including the Maine state police), daytime television drama, and the world in general and would, in addition, keep Dr. Pierce from ever again referring to the governor by his Christian name.

"But I'm going to make one lousy actor, Governor," Steven Harris said. "You know that as well as I do."

"Who'll be able to tell?' the governor said. "And now I'd like to ask another favor of you."

"You politicians never really get enough, do you?"

"This is a rather delicate matter, Trooper Harris," the governor said, sitting up straight in his chair, "involving the very future of our nation."

"I have a personal policy, Governor," Harris replied, "of never making political contributions."

"Would you be surprised to hear that the secretary of state telephoned me earlier today?"

"After what's happened to me in the past couple of days, nothing would surprise me," Harris replied.

"Here's the bottom line," the governor said. "And what you hear within this room, you leave within this room. *Kapish?*"

"Yes, sir," Trooper Harris said. He could tell the governor was quite serious.

"I don't know the whole story myself, Harris," the governor said, "but the Abzugian ambassador has been arrested."

"What did he do?" Steve asked. "And while we're at it, what's an Abzugian ambassador? It sounds like something my friend Boris would think up."

"It's a country. The secretary of state himself assured me of that. He called up and asked me, in the interests of the nation, to pardon this character."

"For what?"

"I don't know," the governor said. "But I went along. Here's the pardon. By the authority invested in me as Governor of Maine, I herewith grant full and absolute pardon to His Excellency Sheikh El Noil Sniol the Magnificent."

"That was a very nice thing for you to do, sir," Harris said.

"I thought so," the governor replied. "But there's one small problem."

"Yes, sir?"

"You know that nebbish O'Flaherty?'

"You mean Warden Patrick O'Flaherty, sir?"

"That's him. Would you believe that he can't find this Abzugian character in his slammer? Now I ask you, how many Abzugians can he possibly have in the slammer? It's not as if I asked him to find and spring one Irishman, from all our Irishmen, or one Italian, from all our Italians. That would pose certain problems. But an Abzugian, especially one with a name like El Noil Sniol, you'd think he'd be able to lay his hands right on him."

"Yes, sir," Harris agreed, "you would. What is it you would like me to do, Governor?"

"On your way back to Spruce Harbor, how 'bout swinging by the slammer and finding this guy for me? Your governor would be grateful."

"What do I do with him?"

"Take him to the Spruce Harbor slammer and leave him there. I'll take it from there."

"Yes, sir," Trooper Harris said.

"Remember," the governor said, "the motto of the Maine state police. We always get our man."

Neither the governor nor Trooper Harris, of course, could have had any way of knowing that three hours before, two men had climbed out of a rented car before the stark gray walls of the state prison, pushed the door buzzer, and demanded entrance.

A somewhat bored guard finally appeared.

"Which one is the guard?" he asked. "And which the guardee?"

"My good man," said Waldo Maldemer, "you err in your snap assessment of the situation. Neither of us is a guard, or alternatively, a guardee. We are, instead, representatives of that bastion of democracy and all-around boon to mankind, electronic media journalism."

"No fooling?"

"I am . . . don't I look and sound familiar? . . . beloved Waldo Maldemer, and this is my trusted associate, Edgar Crudd."

"Am I supposed to recognize you? I mean, is your picture in the post office, or what?"

"My dear man," Waldo said, getting a little red in the jowls, "the time for pretense is past. We *know!*"

"What do you know?"

"That Boris Alexandrovich Korsky-Rimsakov is being held within these gray prison walls."

"Visiting hours are Saturday and Sunday and every other Tuesday, nine to three," the guard said.

"We wish to see the warden," Waldo said, somewhat huffily.

"The warden's busy just now," the guard said.

"In that case, I'll rephrase," Waldo said. "I demand to see the warden."

"Wait a minute," the guard said and slammed the little hole in the door. This somewhat discomfited Waldo Maldemer, who wasn't used to having doors in prison gates slammed in his face, but there didn't seem to be much he could do about it at the moment. He would bide his time until he got to the bottom of this story; *then* he would get him, and get him good. The whole Maine state prison system would get one of the world-famous Waldo Maldemer sneers. Probably a sneer, a raised eyebrow, and the final touch, the Waldo Maldemer inflection-of-voice. They would pay for slamming the slammer door in the face of Waldo Maldemer!

The guard, meanwhile, was on the telephone to Mr. Patrick O'Flaherty.

"Couple of kooks out here, Warden, looking for some guy with a really weird name."

"What's the name?"

The little door opened. "What was that name?"

"Waldo Maldemer," Waldo Maldemer promptly replied.

"I mean the name of the guy who's supposed to be in here."

"Boris Alexandrovich Korsky-Rimsakov," Edgar Crudd said.

The door slammed shut.

"Boris Alexandrovich Korsky-Rimsakov," the guard repeated the name to the warden.

"That's a weird name all right, but it's not the weird name I need," the warden replied. "Tell them to get lost."

"Yes, sir," the guard said. He had almost hung up when he heard the warden's excited cry. "Hey, wait a minute!"

"Yes, sir," the guard said.

"Could either of these guys pass for an Abzugian ambassador?"

"I couldn't really say, Warden. I ain't never seen an Abzugian ambassador."

"Could either of them pass for any kind of ambassador?"

"The fat one with the low-hung jowls could," the guard said, after a moment's thought. "He's got that sort of dazed look, and talks funny, using words nobody understands."

"And the other one?"

"He's more your undertaker type," the guard said.

"Ask them to come in," the warden said. "Take them to my office and get them something to drink. I'll join you in just a couple of minutes."

The whole left side of the gate of the prison opened.

"Sorry for the delay, gentlemen," the guard said, making a little bow. "Would you please come in?"

"That's better," Waldo Maldemer said, and, with Edgar Crudd trailing along behind him, he marched into the state prison. The whole left side of the gate closed after them.

They were shown into the warden's office and, following the warden's orders, presented with a glass of Leprechaun's Delight, the warden's favorite Irish whiskey. And then that luminary himself joined them.

"Sorry to keep you waiting," the warden said. He carefully sized each man up. "How can the state of Maine slammer be of assistance?"

"We wish to see Boris Alexandrovich Korsky-Rimsakov," Edgar Crudd said.

"What makes you think he's here?" the warden replied.

"We know he's here," Waldo Maldemer said, firmly. "Dr. Benjamin Franklin Pierce himself told us he's here."*

"Hawkeye said that?" The warden and the physician were well known to each other, each in the practice of his chosen profession. "You won't mind if I check that out, will you?"

"Check away," Waldo said, grandly, helping himself to another three fingers of Leprechaun's Delight Irish Whiskey as the warden left the room.

The warden found the conversation with his old buddy Hawkeye simply fascinating. Hawkeye denied flatly ever having sent anyone to the prison or saying that anyone he knew was in the prison.

"You know me better than that, Pat," Hawkeye said. "When my pals are in the slammer, my lips are sealed."

"Then who are these two?" Warden Flaherty replied.

"From the description you have given me, Patrick," Hawkeye replied, "they sound like that team of conmen who have been selling phony Irish Sweepstakes tickets to unsuspecting nuns and innocent parochial school children."

"I could tell the minute I laid me Irish eyes on them, Hawkeye," Warden Flaherty replied, "that they were dishonest scoundrels!"

"You're a pretty good judge of character, are you, Patrick?"

"All we Irish are!" Flaherty replied, modestly. "Some more than others, of course."

"Well, you do what you think you must, Patrick," Hawkeye said. "And top of the morning to you."

---

* This was not exactly the truth. It was a journalistic ploy. What Dr. Pierce had actually said, when Waldo Maldemer had finally gotten him back on the telephone, was, "Why don't you try the state prison?"

The warden hung up the phone and called the chief guard.

"Jones," he said, "this is your warden speaking. Go by Cell Block Three and get 'Doc' Riess, the one who's doing thirty-to-life for knocking customers out with knockout drops in his saloon. Bring him along with you to the hospital pharmacy."

Chapter Fifteen

Zelda Spinopolous was more than a little surprised when the telegram welcoming her to the happy television family of ABS arrived, although it did confirm her suspicions about the level of taste of television executives generally.

Her mother, of course, was thrilled. After spending all of the morning in a beauty parlor, Bonita Granville Spinopolous, wearing sunglasses so that the fans wouldn't recognize her as the mother of America's newest star, boarded an Eastern Airlines flight for New York. The network had arranged for this; it would wine and dine the lady and otherwise seek her counsel for an extended period.

This would keep her off the set. There were going to be enough problems on the set without a stage mother, most of them rooted in the fact that Mr. Wesley St. James had not been shown the tape of his new star flashing her snaggle-toothed smile at the camera and rolling her left eye around. It would be the senior network executive's little surprise for him when she appeared on location to film the first, hour-long special introductory program of "The Code of the Deep Woods."

As soon as the collect call announcing Mrs. Spinopolous' immediate departure for New York had been received, the man in charge of things like this telephoned the new star at her home with a change of plans. Instead of flying to New York, she would be flown directly, by small chartered jet, to the Maine location.

Zelda had not earned her cum laude degrees by accepting defeat. While she realized that not flunking the screen test had been a semidisaster, it wasn't the end of her biological life; there was still hope.

She resurrected the printed cotton dress from the Salvation Army, got out her jar of mascara, and found the half-inch-thick granny glasses. She had forty-five minutes from the time the man from ABS called until the limousine pulled up before the Spinopolous' little thirty-six-room cottage overlooking Lake Michigan, time enough to do a really good makeup job.

Zelda quite naturally presumed that her father was at his office. She had no way of knowing that her loving father was just that. He couldn't face, sober, the thought of his little girl leaving home for the wickedness of the world of the theater. (He had not, he was forced to admit to himself, really been seeking cultural enrichment that night a quarter of a century before when he had gone to Sidney Katz's Maison de Paris in Cicero and met the future Mrs. Spinopolous. He had been, in the quaint cant of the time, beating the bushes for a little quail. It was entirely possible, he realized, that out there in the cold cruel world there were other men who would look at Zelda, his own little duckie-wuckie, as quail.)

So, while his secretary had been telling all callers that Mr. Spinopolous was out at Plant Thirteen, watching a test batch of Chef Pierre's newest frozen delight, Goulash a la Les Hongroise, being run through the ovens, Mr. Gus Spinopolous had in fact been in the basement recreation room of his humble home, soaking up ouzo, a licorice-flavored potable he imported from his cousin Sid in Athens. He hadn't even dressed to go to work. He had been virtually sleepless the night before, tormented by the knowledge that this was the last night his little duckie-wuckie would be spending under the familial roof. He had given up trying to sleep at half past five, rolled out of bed, and put on a pair of rather disreputable khaki pants and a sweat shirt emblazoned with the message "CHIEF PIERRE FREEZES FOR YOU!"

which garment had been part of a spectacularly unsuccessful advertising campaign.

He could see out of the basement recreation room and thus had seen his bride of the past quarter century roll off in the blue Rolls. And he saw the black Cadillac limousine roll up and the neatly dressed, rather good-looking young man jump nimbly from the back seat and go up the stairs.

He pushed the downstairs butler's number on the intercom.

"If anybody should ask, Herman," Gus Spinopolous said, "I ain't home."

"I understand, sir. The rather tacky little limousine, if that is the source of your concern, is here to take Miss Zelda . . . pardon me, *Miss Daphne Covington* . . . to the airfield."

"Thanks, Herman," Gus said. He refilled his ouzo glass, drained it, refilled it, and then went to the window again, steeling himself for the sight of his little duckie-wuckie leaving home and hearth. He told himself that he wouldn't cry. Miss Daphne Covington, made up, came down the stairs on the arm of the young man from ABS–Chicago. Gus realized suddenly that his snap judgment of him was wrong. If there had been a sex-crazed maniac, devoting his life to the ruination of young girls, one was coming down the stairway now with his duckie-wuckie on his arm, leering wickedly at her.

He cursed himself then, loudly, not only for sending duckie-wuckie into the world with his paternal protection but, selfish father that he was, for getting so snockered on the ouzo that it looked to him as if his duckie-wuckie was missing a couple of teeth and had big black bags under her eyes.

"Stop!" he shouted, but it was too late. The Cadillac rolled out of the drive.

Gus, first stopping to grab a fresh bottle of ouzo from the case, rushed upstairs.

"Herman!" he bellowed. The butler appeared. "Did

you notice anything about duckie-wuckie, anything strange?"

'I . . . uh . . . took the liberty of inquiring of Miss Daphne Covington, sir, if there was anything amiss. Because of her appearance, sir"

"And? What did she say?"

"Her exact words, sir, were 'You're sweet for worrying, Herman, but don't. This is the way I'm going to look for the rest of my theatrical career.' "

"And did you see the sex maniac with her?"

"Indeed, I did, sir," Herman, highly indignant, said. "While he was waiting for Miss Daphne Covington, he made an indecent proposal to the assistant gardener."

"Did she say where she was going to be staying in New York, Herman?"

"I happened to overhear, quite by accident, sir, when ABS called, that Miss Daphne Covington is not going to New York. She is being flown, by chartered aircraft, to some place called Spruce Harbor, Maine."

"Is there a car here, Herman?" Gus asked. "I sent the green Rolls to the factory so the Missus would think I was gone."

"I believe the red Rolls is here, sir, and of course the yellow Rolls, the Corniche convertible. The one you gave Miss Daphne Covington for Christmas and which she refused to drive."

"Don't ever let me hear you say that again, Herman," Gus said.

"Don't say 'yellow Corniche convertible,' sir?"

"No, you idiot. Daphne Covington," Gus said.

"I never really liked the sound of that name," Herman said. "Is there any way I might be of service, sir?"

"Call the airport," Gus said. "Tell them I'm on my way. Have them warm up the engines."

"Yes, sir," Herman said. "Which aircraft would you like?"

"The fastest one in the Chef Pierre fleet," Gus said. He rushed for the front door.

Herman, a faithful retainer of the old school, went a

bit beyond his instructions. He not only called the aviation division of Chef Pierre's Frozen Delights, International, scrambling the fastest corporate jet available, but made two other calls. The first was to the Chicago police. He chatted briefly with a deputy commissioner, reminding him how long and how well the political fortunes of the mayor had been supported by his good friend Gus Spinopolous, and then informing him that Mr. Spinopolous was at that moment rushing to the airport in a yellow Corniche convertible on pressing personal family business. Within moments, the word flashed over the police radio. The convertible was intercepted as Gus reached Lake Shore Drive. Two motorcycle cops, sirens screaming, caught up with the car, pulled abreast, waved at the driver in a friendly way, and then pulled ahead. They turned on their flashing lights and cleared the way.

Traffic all along Lake Shore Drive had, of course, already been stopped. As Gus, preceded by the motorcycle cops, raced along it, other police vehicles, lights flashing, sirens and whoopers whooping, joined the procession. As they passed the traffic policemen barring traffic at intersections, these minions of the law saluted crisply.

It was all accomplished with practiced skill and efficiency. They did this all the time, of course, for His Honor the Mayor, when the boss had to go to an Irish wake, or a Bonds for Israel dinner, or a Hungarian hoedown, and they were perfectly happy to do it for any close personal friend of His Honor's, whose number was apparently legion.

The procession reached Lake Front airport. Sitting on the threshold of the active runway was a Sabreliner bearing the familiar logotype of Chef Pierre's smiling Gallic face on the nose; its engines were whistling softly.

The Rolls skidded to a stop. Gus Spinopolous, a bottle of ouzo (from which he had taken several large nips en route to steady his nerves) in his hand, jumped out

toss down three fingers of Leprechaun's Delight, "to the Spruce Harbor Jail."

"And I've already called me good friend Chief Ernie Kelly, a fellow officer of the Friendly Sons of Saint Patrick, and told him what to expect," Warden O'Flaherty said. "And he said he'd be waiting for you."

"Thank you very much," Harris said.

"Have another nip," the warden said. "Tell me, Harris, how come I never saw you at one gathering or another of the Friendly Sons?"

"I don't belong to the Friendly Sons," Harris said.

"Come on! A great big ugly buck of a lad like you, and ye'r not in the Friendly Sons? Now, how can that be?"

"I'm an Englishman," Harris said, without thinking. "Or my parents were."

The glass he was about to raise to his lips was snatched from his hands.

"There'll be no drinking on duty when Warden O'Flaherty's around," he said. "Englishman, indeed! It's a good thing they've thrown you off the force, you disgrace to policeman's blue, or I'd have to arrange that myself."

The warden carefully repoured the three fingers of Leprechaun's Delight back into the bottle, turned on his heel, and marched across the prison yard to his office. Steven Harris turned and looked at his car. The two Abzugians, both of whom looked vaguely familiar somehow, were propped up on the back seat, mouths open, snoring in harmony.

Steven Harris got behind the wheel, started the engine, and drove out of the Maine state slammer.

Chief Ernie Kelly of the Spruce Harbor Police Department thought of himself as the finest of Spruce Harbor's finest. If he wasn't, he reasoned, obviously someone else would be chief and get to wear the chief's hat . . . which was actually a helmet. The helmet was left with Chief Kelly by a friendly salesman of the Peace, Law, and Order Equipment Company as an absolutely free, no-strings-attached gift. It was dark blue in color and had, in addition to a clear-plastic face mask and a leather strap for the chin, a short-wave antenna rising from its center and a microphone boom fixed to the side dangling the mike itself before the chief's mouth. It said "CHIEF" in large gold letters on the front, a burst of lightning bolts was portrayed on each side, and the word "POLICE" was printed on the back, presumably to reassure the citizenry that the wearer had not come from Mars.

The salesman, of course, had believed that such a device would be absolutely irresistible as an item of police equipment and that he could shortly expect an order for thirty-six similar items to fully equip the active (twelve men) and reserve (twenty-four men) police forces of the Spruce Harbor Department of Public Safety and Sanitation, at the special three-dozen price of $109.75 each.

No such order was forthcoming, although Chief Kelly had indeed presented himself before the City Council in his helmet to make such a request. All the chief had gotten for his trouble was the sight of the entire City Council, to a man, bent double in hysterics.

Chief Kelly, however, continued to wear his helmet on any occasion when he thought he could get away with it. He frankly didn't understand why everyone thought it was so funny. If the state police could march around wearing their Smokey-the-Bear hats, with no one laughing at them, what was so funny about him wearing the helmet?

The police department today was on full mobilization, which is to say that all leaves had been canceled and the reserves mobilized, which meant that no garbage would be collected until further notice, the garbagemen having been called to duty to preserve the peace of Spruce Harbor against the threat presented by the following:

(a) The temporary incarceration, at the request of

the governor himself, in the Spruce Harbor slammer of an international criminal, El Noil Sniol, until

(b)   the arrival of the secretary of state, who would take (a) off his hands;

(c)   the arrival from Hollywood, California, of Miss Patience Throckbottom Worthington, beloved star of stage, screen, and daytime television drama, who would occupy Room 19 of the Spruce Harbor Howard Hilton Motor Hotel until her dressing room could be imported from California;

(d)   the arrival, from Chicago, of Miss Daphne Covington, described as television's newest, brightest star;

(e)   the arrival of Mr. Wesley St. James and his production crew for the new Wesley St. James daytime drama, "The Code of the Deep Woods."

Chief Kelly was determined to milk this fortuitous circumstance for all it was worth. He was personally involved with it, rather than just professionally, and for a number of reasons.

He was sick and tired of seeing what he thought of as "relatively smaller" police departments maligned on boob-tube cops-and-robbers shows. They were invariably portrayed as backwoods dumbbells who had to be rescued from their own stupidity and incompetence by big city cops who just happened to be in town. (He was sure of his facts. He considered it his professional obligation to watch all the television police shows, and he had made copious notes. The only rural law-enforcement officer on television who ever got his man without the help of some city slicker was Matt Dillon, and his show, naturally, had been canceled.)

Chief Kelly had carefully planned the way his force would handle this day's problems. The big event, crimewise, was the Abzugian criminal El Noil Sniol. He would make sure not only that this international felon was securely incarcerated in his slammer but also that the world would know about it.

To this end, he had been in touch with the local television station and coordinated the schedule of their ace (and only) cameraman, Ace Marshutz. Marshutz would be on hand at the city jail when El Noil Sniol arrived. After filming that, he would be carried by official city vehicle to Spruce Harbor International Airport for the arrival of Miss Patience T. Worthington, Miss Daphne Covington, and Mr. Wesley St. James. He would capture on film the perfectly professional security arrangements Chief Kelly had set up for the arrival of the secretary of state and would finally film the transfer of El Noil Sniol to the secretary of state's security people.

ABS Television News, with whom he had talked long distance to New York, was fascinated. "The Code of the Deep Woods" was, after all, going to be telecast over the ABS network, and if a little teensy-weensy plug for the show could be worked in as legitimate news, that was just fine. Chief Kelly told the ABS people he would see what he could do about getting Miss Worthington to the ceremony transferring El Noil Sniol to the secretary of state, but could, of course, make no promises.

The only thing that threatened to pose an insurmountable problem to Chief Kelly's carefully laid plans was the Honorable Bascomb K. Bartlett, mayor of Spruce Harbor and more widely known as "Moosenose." Like any other politician, Moosenose was thrilled with the thought of seeing himself on television and, once word of what was about to happen in his fair city had reached him, had declared himself in.

He would, he said: (a) Be at the slammer when El Noil Sniol arrived; (b) be at the airport to officially welcome the visiting dignitaries; and (c) if Ernie Kelly didn't like it, Ernie Kelly could lump it.

Chapter Sixteen

And so it came to pass, as it says in the Good Book, that when State Trooper Steven J. Harris rolled up in his patrol car before the Spruce Harbor City Hall and slammer, he was greeted by two official functionaries, the Spruce Harbor High School Drum and Bugle Corps and a representative of television journalism, whose equipment had been set up on a Spruce Harbor garbage truck.

Chief Kelly was there, of course, in full uniform, the visor down on his helmet and in instantaneous communication with the police radio via the short-wave set in the helmet. Mayor Moosenose Bartlett was in morning dress—a high silk hat, penguin-tailed coat, and striped trousers—and had a purple velvet band (obtained from the Spruce Harbor Flower and Gift Shoppe) across his chest spelling out "MAYOR" in four-inch gold letters.

"Rolling!" Ace Marshutz, the photographer, called. Somewhat nervously (this would be his first appearance on nationwide television), Cordell Carlsbad, the local anchorman, fixed a smile on his face and started talking:

"Hi, folks," he said. "This is Cordell Carlsbad speaking to you live from the steps of Spruce Harbor City Hall, where the international criminal, El Noil Sniol, will shortly be transferred into the custody of our own Chief Ernie Kelly. That black and white automobile you see on your screens now, with the siren and flashing light device on the roof, is a police car, used in cases like this by the police."

Ignoring everybody, Steven J. Harris opened the rear

183

door of his patrol car, grabbed the rear shirt collar of one prisoner in his right hand, the rear shirt collar of the other prisoner in his left hand, and half carried them, half dragged them, up the stairs to where Ernie Kelly stood, arms folded on his chest, a look of stern resolve on his face, waiting.

The Spruce Harbor High School Drum and Bugle Corps struck up "Oh, Fair Spruce Harbor!" (which fortunately had the same tune as that used by the University of Notre Dame).

Both Mayor Bartlett and Chief Kelly knew that they needed something more than film of two unconscious people (for all the world, they looked like two common drunks) being dragged up the city hall steps. They rushed to assist Trooper Harris, propped the two criminals up on their feet between them, and turned them to face the camera.

"Which one is El Noil Sniol?" Chief Kelly hissed from behind his face shield.

"The fat one with the jowls," Harris replied. "What's going on, Ernie?"

"Spruce Harbor is proud," His Honor the Mayor said, beaming at Ace Marshutz's camera, "to have been chosen to incarcerate these international criminals in its well-known, very modern, and rather appealing city jail, which, with all modesty, I must admit was constructed during my administration."

The fat one with the jowls, as Trooper Harris had described him, stirred and opened his eyes. He saw the television camera and the glowing light, indicating that he was being "shot." He had no idea where he was, or what he was doing here, but he had faced that precise situation before, and it posed no problem.

"Good evening," he said. "This is Waldo Maldemer. We'll give you this story in just a moment. But first, this commercial message!"

The effort was too much for him. With a smile on his face, his eyes closed again. The sound of his voice, however, woke Edgar Crudd up. He too saw the camera and the glowing red light, and he too performed like a trouper, even though he had even less of an idea than did Mr. Maldemer of what was going on. The last thing he remembered was being encouraged to take another drink at the Maine state slammer.

"Edgar Crudd here," he said, staring intently at the camera. "And now back to you, Waldo Maldemer!" Then he too gave up the ghost and sagged between Trooper Harris and Mayor Moosenose Bartlett.

Cordell Carlsbad, aware that this might be his chance to break into the big time, had paid no attention whatever to what the mayor, Waldo Maldemer, or Edgar Crudd had been saying. He was thinking of how to close this story.

"And that's the way it is," he finally blurted at Ace Marshutz's camera. "Here at the Spruce Harbor slammer. I am Cordell Carlsbad."

The red light blinked off on Ace's camera. Four reserve policemen emerged from the city hall building, and with the same flair and élan with which they normally tossed about Spruce Harbor's garbage cans, picked up Waldo and Edgar and carried them into the building and to the basement jail.

Mayor Moosenose Bartlett, allowing the warm smile to slip from his face, cocked his head to one side like a cocker spaniel and then peered into the sky.

"My God!" he said. "That's a jet! We have to get to the airport right now!"

He rushed down the stairs and jumped into the chief of police's car. Chief Kelly got behind the wheel, started the engine, and turned on the whooper. Carried away with the excitement of it all, Reserve Policeman Harry Whelan (normally a garbage truck driver) threw his garbage truck in gear and raced after the chief's car. He left so rapidly that he quite forgot cameraman Ace Marshutz, who was standing on top. Ace came tumbling down. Steve Harris saw him fall in time to catch him

(Ace weighed 113 pounds with his headset) and set him on his feet.

"Be a good guy, Steve," Ace asked. "Run me down to the airport, will you?"

Steve and Ace got into the state police car and drove off toward the airport. Two blocks from city hall, Trooper Harris saw a Spruce Harbor Medical Center ambulance obviously bound for the airport. He pulled alongside to see if he could offer any professional assistance. He was somewhat surprised to see that the driver was Dr. John Francis Xavier McIntyre and that the seat normally occupied by the other ambulance technician was occupied by Dr. Benjamin Franklin Pierce. On Dr. Pierce's lap was Chief of Nursing Services Esther Flanagan.

"Can I help?" Harris called from his police car. "Is there some sort of a disaster?"

"We hope not," Trapper John called back. "But just to play safe, would you be good enough to escort us near the airplane that's going to land in a couple of minutes?"

"You got it!" Harris said. He reached up and turned on his whooper and flashing blue lights, pulled in front of the ambulance, and stepped on the gas.

Drs. Pierce and McIntyre had just been informed by Wrong Way Napolitano of the pending arrival of a Chevaux Corporation jet. While Wrong Way was not in the habit of making special private announcements of the arrival of aircraft to the public, he was now doing so in the interest of domestic tranquillity on the part of his brother Angelo, a/k/a Pierre LeGrande, and his wife. Dr. Pierce had pointed out to him that if Angelo's wife learned that Angelo had been out in the deep woods with Mr. Wesley St. James's friends, she would remember that Angelo and the ladies had been flown into the deep woods by Wrong Way, and he would ipso facto be considered an accessory before and after (and quite possibly during) the act.

Angelo, at that very moment, was very busy in the control tower. Never before had there been so much traffic, all homing in on Spruce Harbor International Airport* at once.

"Ah, Spruce Harbor International," the pilot of the Chevaux Petroleum DC-9 said, "Chevaux Thirty-two has turned on final, but all I have in sight is what looks like a country road. Where's the airport?"

"Spruce Harbor International," Wrong Way replied, "clears Chevaux Thirty-two to land on Spruce Harbor Runway One."

"Spruce Harbor International," another pilot's voice said. "This is Los Angeles Charter Airways. We have Miss Patience T. Worthington aboard, and we have Chevaux Petroleum Corporation DC-9 in sight, making a descent. Request landing instructions."

"Spruce Harbor clears Los Angeles Charter Airways as Number Two to land after the Chevaux Petroleum DC-9," Angelo replied.

"Spruce Harbor International, this is Chef Pierre Number Sixteen, five miles from your station," a third pilot's voice said. "You're not going to believe this, but this aircraft has in sight a DC-9 and a Learjet making a landing approach on a country road."

"Spruce Harbor International clears Chef Pierre Number Sixteen as Number Three to land, after the Learjet. And just for your information, Chef Pierre, that country road you're talking about is Spruce Harbor Runway One."

"Spruce Harbor," still another crisp, machismo-loaded pilot's voice announced, "this is Air Force Three. We have the secretary of state aboard. Please clear all traffic from the area so that we may land immediately."

---

* The name might be misleading. Before a Whiz-Bang Airways DC-3, en route from Bangor to Montreal, had run low on fuel and dropped in on Spruce Harbor's one-runway flight facility, it had been known as the Napolitano Truck Farm and Crop Spraying Service. Once an international flight had actually landed on the field, however, the Spruce Harbor Chamber of Commerce had been quick to change the official name of the facility to reflect its proper role in international air commerce. Only an innate sense of modesty had made them refrain from renaming the airport the Spruce Harbor Aerospace Launching Pad, as was proposed.

"Air Force Three, hold in pattern," Wrong Way replied immediately.

"Spruce Harbor, this is Air Force Three. I say again, we have the secretary of state aboard and demand immediate permission to land."

"Air Force Three, this is Spruce Harbor. I say again, hold in pattern. I don't care if you have the governor of Maine aboard."

"Spruce Harbor," said a pilot's voice in the peculiar twang of Downeast, "this is Maine National Guard One. I have the governor aboard. Request permission to land immediately."

"Spruce Harbor, this is Chevaux Number Thirty-two, on the ground at five past the hour."

"Chevaux Thirty-two, do you have a certain lady aboard?" Wrong Way asked, at the request of His Honor Mayor Moosenose Bartlett, who had joined him in the control tower.

"Oh, do we ever!" Chevaux Thirty-two replied.

"His Honor the Mayor will meet your aircraft," Wrong Way said.

The mayor rushed from the control tower, getting a nasty splinter in his hand from the wooden ladder, and jumped into Chief Kelly's car. "It's the first one," he said. "Just think, Ernie, sweet saintly Patience T. Worthington is going to be here in Spruce Harbor, officially greeted by me!"

By then, the Spruce Harbor High School Drum and Bugle Corps had arrived in their bus, and they followed the chief's car and the "camera truck" down the field to where the Chevaux DC-9 was rolling to a stop.

"Spruce Harbor, Los Angeles Charter on the ground at six past the hour," the pilot reported.

"Spruce Harbor," said Wrong Way, who knew on which side his bread was buttered, "clears Maine National Guard One to land after the Chef Pierre Sabreliner now on final."

"But the secretary of state outranks the governor of Maine!" the pilot of Air Force Three said, angrily.

"Not in Maine, he don't," Spruce Harbor International replied. "Welcome to Spruce Harbor, Governor!"

Meanwhile, the door of Chevaux Petroleum Corporation's aircraft had opened. A set of aluminum stairs unfolded itself, and then a female appeared at the doorway. The Spruce Harbor High School Drum and Bugle Corps struck up "Oh, Fair Spruce Harbor."

The female was wearing a light purple dress, full length but cut rather low at the neckline. Over her shoulders was a blue-and-red cape. She carried in her right hand a large, gold-painted pole, the top of which was curved to make sort of a handle. Around her neck was a golden cross, approximately ten inches in length, on which was spelled out in diamond chips, the words "Mother" and "Emeritus" (horizontally) and "Reverend" vertically.

Moosenose stared, mouth hanging open at this apparition, for a moment. The lady turned, and one could see the same legend spelled out in diamonds on the cross spelled out in sequin letters on the back of the cape.

"I come in peace!" the lady said, raising both of her arms upward in a gesture frequently used by politicians. In her case, however, the movement caused her upper torso to move in such a manner that the immediate escape, so to speak, of her bosom seemed inescapable.

"Ernie," Moosenose said, out of the side of his mouth, "that don't look like Patience Throckbottom Worthington to me."

"You there," the lady said, "with the mayor sign on your boiled shirt."

"Yes, ma'am?" Moosenose replied, tipping his hat.

"Reverend Mother to you, Mayor," the lady said.

"Yes, ma'am, Reverend Mother," His Honor said. sweating profusely. "What can I do for you?"

"What have you done with my pal Boris?" the lady inquired.

"Hey, Hot Lips!" a familiar voice, one Moosenose and the lady simultaneously recognized to be that of Dr.

Benjamin Franklin Pierce, called out. Both looked toward the ambulance.

The double doors were now open. The stretchers had been removed, and the floor was covered with shag carpet. There was a wine cooler and a tray of glasses. There was the sound of a popping cork. Boris Alexandrovich Korsky-Rimsakov took the bottle from Nurse Flanagan and waved it gaily in the air.

"Oh," the lady cried, "you didn't have to do this for Little Ol' Reverend Mother!" She trotted down the stairs and, hiking her skirts up, ran across the grass to the ambulance. She got inside the ambulance. Before the doors closed and the ambulance pulled away, Moosenose heard the lady say, "Darling, you've shaved! You look awful!"

At this moment, Chef Pierre Number Sixteen, which had been third to land, stopped rolling. Its door opened and Gus Spinopolous, still dressed in his CHEF PIERRE FREEZES FOR YOU! sweat shirt and clutching a fresh bottle of ouzo, sort of lurched out onto the runway. He shook his head as if to clear it and then ran over to Moosenose.

"Was she on that plane?" he demanded.

"Was who on that plane?"

"Zelda Spinopolous, you idiot, who else?"

"Lock this drunk up, Ernie," Moosenose said. "Whatever would Miss Patience T. Worthington think if she saw a drunk running loose around our fair city?"

Chief Kelly spoke to his helmet radio, and a squad of the police reserve came running out to haul the drunk off to durance vile. About half way to where Gus Spinopolous stood, weaving somewhat, they encountered the six worthies from the warehouse of Plant Number Forty-three, Shrimp and Oysters, who had seen Ol' Gus's plane (they recognized it from the Chef Pierre insignia on the nose, of course) land. The two squads of men ran along parallel, in step, until they reached the mayor, the chief, and Ol' Gus.

"Yes, Chief?" the squad leader reported, snappily.

"Anything we can do, Gus?" the warehouse foreman asked.

"They've got my Zelda somewhere, and they won't tell me what they've done with her," Gus said, as a tear ran down his cheek.

"Book him," Chief Kelly said, sternly. "Drunk, disorderly, disturbing the peace, and giving Spruce Harbor a bad name."

"If you know what's good for you, pal," the warehouse foreman said to His Honor the Mayor, "you better give ol' Gus's Zelda back!"

Chief Kelly checked to see that the light on Ace Marshutz's television camera was glowing brightly. "Book all of 'em!" he said, flipping up the face visor on his helmet, so that Ace could see his face, stern with resolve.

That was a sort of tactical error, resulting in what Chief Kelly would thereafter refer to as his wound on the field of battle. Gus Spinopolous reached inside the helmet and grabbed Chief Kelly's proboscis between his thumb and forefinger and twisted it painfully. The chief howled loud enough to attract the attention of a second squad of police reservists, who came at the run and subdued the warehouse staff and Mr. Spinopolous; not, however, without some difficulty.

While the fight was going on, other aircraft landed practically unnoticed. First the governor's plane, then the secretary of state's, then (swooping in like a graceful vulture) the *Le Discorde* carrying the sheikh of Abzug, and finally a small jet carrying Miss Daphne Covington.

Miss Covington, truth to tell, had rather enjoyed the flight from Chicago. The exquisitely graceful young man from ABS had been a delightful traveling companion. Daphne had spent most of the flight rolling her left eye at him and every once in a while granting him a snaggletoothed smile and a leering wink. Once, over upper New York State, she thought that he was about to jump out of the airplane, and she was afraid she had gone too far, but he lost his resolve at the last moment and spent the balance of the flight curled up in a corner whimpering. The moment the plane landed at Spruce Harbor, however, he pushed open the door and jumped to the ground and ran away.

Daphne arrived, in other words, to find no one waiting for her. She walked up toward the main building of the airport, practicing her limp. Her spirits were high. Judging by the reaction of the exquisitely graceful young man from ABS, it would only be a matter of hours before she would be free to return to Chicago and her microscope.

When she had limped up to the Spruce Harbor International Airfield Terminal Building, she had no trouble making her way through the crowds of people who were cheering one side or another in a monumental brawl or staring goggle-eyed at a curly-haired gentleman in robes and the governor of Maine. All she had to do was roll her left eye, and the crowds parted before her as if by magic.

Only one person didn't recoil with revulsion and horror in his eyes when Daphne's eye rolled at him. This was an enormous state trooper who seemed to be trying very hard, and slowly succeeding, to bring order out of the chaos. Shortly after separating the governor and the secretary of state, who were engaged in a little shoving match and the exchange of impolite comments, the trooper walked directly over to her. Testing her powers, Daphne rolled her eye as best she could, smiled her snaggle-toothed smile, and dropped her right eyebrow in the same sort of obscene wink that had driven the man from ABS quite literally bananas. It had no effect at all on the trooper.

"I've got my hands full at the moment, miss," he said, politely touching his hand to his Smokey-the-Bear hat, "but I will soon have things under control and will then be able to assist you. If you'll just wait here, everything will be all right."

He then returned to the secretary of state, the Arab gentleman, and the governor. Daphne, somewhat ashamed that her female curiosity was getting the best of her, limped closer so that she could hear what was going on.

A police van rolled onto the airfield. A policeman wearing a Martian helmet came running up from the far end of the field, where several large aircraft were parked. His face was flushed, and he was obviously out of breath as he was determined to do his duty. He went to the rear of the van, flung the doors open, and with the help of two policemen dragged two handcuffed figures, who gave every appearance of having sniffed too long at a wine cork, from the interior.

He marched them up to the governor, the secretary of state, and the Arab gentleman. He saluted.

"Sir," he said, as the taller of the two criminals sagged and the fat one with the hanging jowls slipped to the ground, "the Spruce Harbor Police Force, Chief Ernest Kelly commanding, turns over to you herewith the international criminal El Noil Sniol and his henchman."

"He's not an international criminal, you idiot," the secretary of state said. "He's the Distinguished Abzugian Ambassador Plenipotentiary. Get the cuffs off him!"

"Who are these two funny-looking people?" the Arab gentleman asked. He spoke in Yiddish. He spoke no English, and the secretary spoke no Arabic. They had long ago learned to communicate in Yiddish, a lingua franca in which both were fluent.

"He's your ambassador extraordinary and plenipotentiary, that's who he is," the secretary said. "I have arranged with His Excellency the Governor to have him pardoned."

"Never saw either one of 'em before," Sheikh Abdullah said. "But goniffs they surely are."

"Sheikh Abdullah, Governor," the secretary of state replied, "tells me this is not El Noil Sniol the Magnificent. You got maybe an explanation?"

"Trooper Harris?" the governor snapped.

"These are the two I got from the warden," Harris replied.

"Put the handcuffs back on and take them back to the slammer," the governor ordered. "I can see that O'Flaherty's been at the Leprechaun's Delight again."

"Yes, sir," Chief Kelly said. "I'm sorry, Governor."

The governor ignored him. He turned to Harris. "Have you got a car, Harris?"

"Yes, sir," Harris said.

"Only one man could be responsible for this chaos," the governor said. "The whole thing smacks of one of his well-known assaults on society. I want you to take us to a doctor named Pierce, Harris. Can you find him?"

"Maybe you're not so backward after all," the secretary said.

"Yes, sir, I can find him," Harris said. "But, sir, I must take someone else with us."

"Who?"

"That beautiful young lady over there," Harris said, pointing directly at Daphne Covington. She was so startled that it was a moment before she remembered to roll her eye.

The secretary of state covered his eyes with his hand.

"You call dat a beautiful young lady?" he asked. *"Oy vay!"* .

"I judge a book not by its cover, Mr. Secretary," Harris said, "but by its contents. I can tell by her eyes that she is a beautiful person. And I know that she is friendless."

"She can ride in front with you," the governor said. "Tell her not to turn around."

Daphne Covington flushed bright red in embarrassment as the trooper came and gently took her arm and led her to the police car and installed her in the front seat. She wondered why she was letting herself be led around like this. She also wondered if this handsome law-enforcement officer was spoken for.

Chapter Seventeen

Miss Patience Throckbottom Worthington, whose plane had landed second, had taken one look out the window and decided that she had no intention whatever of getting off the airplane. Some sacrifices, certainly, were necessary in the pursuit of one's theatrical career, but there had to be a line drawn somewhere, and she had just drawn it.

She would have ordered the plane back into the air, but that would have denied her the great pleasure of discussing her displeasure with Mr. Wesley St. James. The bleeping little blap was really going to get a bleeping earful. She called for another little sip of Old White Stagg Kentucky Bourbon and looked out the window again as she delicately tipped the half-gallon bottle to her lips.

"Well," she said to no one in particular, "they aren't all savages!"

She had just seen the Spruce Harbor Medical Center ambulance doors swing open and the jeroboam of champagne being uncorked.

"And there," she went on, as Boris waved the bottle at Hot Lips, "is my handsome co-star! He looks even better in the flesh."

Then a frown crossed her soft features, quickly turning her face into one of deep annoyance. She had seen Reverend Mother Emeritus Margaret Houlihan Wachauf Wilson leap nimbly into the ambulance, kiss *her*, Patience T. Worthington's, co-star on the cheeks, and then pull the door closed, with something obviously far more intimate on her mind.

"And with *my* co-star!" Patience exploded. "I have changed my mind. Open the doors!"

"I'm afraid we can't do that, Miss Worthington," the stewardess replied.

"Listen, coffee, tea, and milk," Miss Worthington snapped, "when Patience T. Worthington says open the bleeping doors, you bleeping well better open the bleeping doors!"

"Very well, Miss Worthington," the stewardess replied. "Watch your step!"

There is reason to believe that the stewardess knew full well the ramp had not been placed again on the airplane and that the one step to the ground about which she thoughtfully warned Miss Worthington was some twenty-two feet in height, but there is, of course, no way to prove it.

In any event, Miss Worthington exited the airplane, sans ramp, and the next thing she remembered she was looking up into the somewhat flushed face of a man with a strangely shaped proboscis.

"Moosenose," she said, a little groggily.

"Miss Worthington," His Honor replied. "You know my name?"

Miss Worthington thereupon screamed in pain.

"Oh, Miss Worthington," Moosenose asked. "Is something the matter?"

"You bleeping jackass," Miss Worthington replied, "of course something is the matter. I have broken my bleeping leg. Why the bleep did you think I let out that bleeping scream? To call my mate? Get an ambulance, and get one bleeping quick!"

Mayor Bartlett at that point fainted. It wasn't the sight of the broken leg but rather the language. His cherished dream of thirty-five years was just as shattered as Miss Worthington's femur. Attracted by the sound of Miss Worthington's piquant language, however, others came, and an ambulance was called. Both were hauled away in it. Moosenose thus realized his dream of sleeping beside Patience Throckbottom Worthington, even if not precisely how he had hoped it would be.

The arrival of Miss Patience Throckbottom Worthington at Spruce Harbor Medical Center broke up the festivities then in progress in the office of the chief of surgery. The chief of surgery, the chief of nursing services, and Dr. McIntyre expressed their deep regrets at having to answer the call of duty and suggested that under the circumstances Boris take Hot Lips out to Trooper Harris' cabin in the swamp buggy. They would join them there as soon as they could.

As Boris drove away from the rear entrance of Spruce Harbor Medical Center in the swamp buggy, the secretary of state, the governor, and Sheikh Abdullah ben Abzug drove up to the front. In two minutes the governor came back out. He motioned Trooper Harris out of the car, so that the pathetic creature with him wouldn't hear what he had to say.

"Both of those maniacs are in surgery," the governor said. "They told me that, and I didn't believe it, so they showed me. But they're responsible for all this, and they can't hide out in there forever. You get on the radio, Harris, and have my car and driver sent down here. You better have them send the helicopter, too. And then . . . I hate to ask you to do this . . . you take that pathetic creature somewhere, hide her from public sight, and as soon as I get to the bottom of this, I'll arrange for the proper kind of care."

"You mean I can go?"

"Just keep her out of sight," the governor said.

Harris walked back to the car, called for the governor's car, driver, and helicopter, and then turned to look at Daphne Covington.

She let him have the rolling eye, the snaggle-toothed smile, and the obscene wink again, and again it didn't work. She was ashamed of herself

"Listen," she said, "I'm not what I seem to be."

"Neither am I," Harris said.

"What do you mean by that?"

"I'm not really a state trooper," he said.

"You sure act like one," she said.

"I was," he said. "I was a good one, too. But something came up, and I got fired."

"Oh, I'm so sorry," she said. "What do you do now? I mean, how come the uniform?"

"This is my last day on the job," he said. "Tomorrow ... tomorrow ..."

"What about tomorrow?"

"I'd rather not talk about it," he said. "I'm ashamed of it."

"Well, I've got a confession to make, too," she said. "I'm here to do something I don't want to do, either."

"What?"

"You ever hear of a man called Wesley St. James?"

She could tell by the shocked look in what she had come to think of as his beautiful baby-blue eyes that he was quite familiar with the name. He nodded his head.

"Well, I'm here to meet him," Daphne Covington said. "Now you know."

"I know where he is," Harris said. "I'll take you to him."

Daphne was a little disappointed, but there was nothing that maidenly modesty would permit her to do about it. She could hardly expect someone she had met an hour before to offer to save her from Wesley St. James and a life on the boards.

They chatted a little on the way to Lost Crystal Lake. They each tactfully elicited from the other that there was "nobody special" on either side, and that their lives to date had been such that there had been no time for real romance. She was about to timidly announce that what she really wanted to do with her life was become an analytical biologist when he pulled off the interstate highway.

"Hold your nose," he said. "We're passing the senator's potato chip factory. It's only a couple of miles from here."

"I was told we'd have to fly in," she said, her voice somewhat nasal with her nostrils pinched shut.

"Lost Crystal Lake is the water supply for the potato chip factory," he said. The road was rough, and there was no further opportunity for conversation. Finally, he stopped the car.

"It's right around the corner," he said. "They've been working in here all week, building the sets."

"Oh," she said. He touched her then for the first time, taking her arm in his massive hand to help her through the woods. She had felt perfectly healthy (a little glum, but healthy) before, but now she was dizzy. In just a few minutes, they were standing on the shore of Lost Crystal Lake. She spotted Wesley St. James, his Australian bush hat pushed back on his blond Afro, talking to some workmen.

"There he is," Steven said.

"Yes," Daphne said.

Daphne realized that she had but one chance now, and that was to get fired right here on the spot. That way, Trooper Harris would feel duty-bound to take care of her, if only to drive her back out of the woods. Daphne Covington gave the greatest (and, as it turned out, the final) performance of her theatrical career.

She limped up to Wesley St. James, and with a final burst of inspiration, thought to lisp as she rolled her left eye at him.

"Hello, Mr. St. James," she said. "I'm Daphne Covington, your new star."

Wesley St. James started to laugh. It was a nasty little laugh.

"I got to hand it to you, Harris," he said. "I never would have thought you'd have a sense of humor like that."

"Like what, Mr. St. James?"

"A practical joke like this," St. James said, between giggles. "Bringing this ugly freak in here and telling me she's my new star."

She was succeeding! Daphne put her whole heart

and soul into it. She saw someone coming, recognized him to be Don Rhotten, America's most beloved young television newscaster (of course, he had his caps, contacts, and toupee in place), and flashed him a quick eye roll, a shy smile, and a leering wink. Don Rhotten stopped in his tracks, turned pale, rolled his own eyes, and threw up.

"Enough!" Wesley St. James said. "A joke is a joke, but you're messing up my set. Get your ugly freak out of here, Harris."

"I think you owe the lady an apology," Trooper Harris said.

"Bleep you and your bleeping apology," Wesley St. James snarled. "My bleeping star broke her bleeping leg, and you bring this bleeping freak in here, make my pal Don Rhotten sick at his tummy, and you want me to apologize? Bleep you, Harris."

He would have said more, but by that time he was describing a neat parabolic arc through the air, terminating in the icy waters of Lost Crystal Lake.

Don Rhotten rushed to his friend's defense. He followed Mr. St. James in aerial flight except that, following the laws of physics, which state that a heavy body retains velocity longer than a light one, he landed somewhat nearer the center of the lake.

"Well," Daphne Covington said, beaming from ear to ear, "there goes the old theatrical career!"

"How did you know?" he said. "Not that it matters, but how did you know that I threw my theatrical career in the lake with those two?"

"*Your* career?" Daphne asked. "What do you mean, your career?" She had a sinking feeling in her stomach that she had just blown her one great romantic opportunity in life.

"I didn't want to be an actor anyway," he said. "Forget it. Come on, let's get out of here."

"Where are we going?" Daphne asked. "Hey, listen. My real name is Zelda."

"Zelda," Steven said. "Gee, that's a pretty name!"

"You really think so?" Zelda said.

"Here," Steven Harris said, "let me take your arm."

They walked arm in arm back to his car and then drove to his log cabin on the lake.

"Hey, Boris is here," Steve said.

"Who's Boris?"

"He's a really nice guy, a little crazy, to tell you the truth, that I'm sort of taking care of."

"Is that so?" Zelda said.

"The thing is, Zelda," Steven Harris said, "I need the money. I'm saving up to go to medical school."

"No kidding?" she said. "I want to be an analytic biologist myself," Zelda said.

"Yeah? Maybe we might be at the same school together."

"That thought crossed my mind," Zelda said.

"You must be Steve Harris," Hot Lips, who had abandoned her theological vestments and was now wearing a bikini, said, stepping to the door of the cabin with a martini glass in her hand.

"Yes, ma'am," Steve said, modestly averting his eyes. "And who are you, ma'am?"

"I'm the Reverend Mother Emeritus Wilson," she said. "My friends call me Hot Lips, and any friend of my pal Boris is a friend of mine." She looked at Zelda. "Honey, I don't want to hurt your feelings, but your mascara has slipped."

"Steve!" Boris said. "Where the hell have you been?" He looked at Zelda. "Hello, sweetie," he said. "I am Boris Alexandrovich Korsky-Rimsakov, the world's greatest opera singer."

"Zelda, ignore him!" Steve hissed.

"What happened to your beard, Mr. Korsky-Rimsakov?" Zelda replied. "I'm one of your greatest fans." She qualified the comment. "Musically, not biologically."

"Where did you find this delightful patroness of the arts, Steve?" Boris asked. Then, remembering: "Hey, they're trying to get you on the radio. Some heiress has been kidnapped. They're offering a million-dollar ranso█ for her."

Zelda winced. "What was the name?" she asked. Th█ would be the sixteenth time her father had mistaken█ reached the conclusion that she had been kidnapped.

"Some wild name. Greek."

"Spinopolous?"

"That's it," Boris said. "How did you know?"

"Stab in the dark," Zelda said.

"I have been talking to Hot Lips about your litt█ problem, Steve."

"Which little problem is that?"

"About getting into medical school."

"It's a lost cause," Steve said. "I can't get in, and █ don't have the money, and I just threw Wesley S█ James into Lost Crystal Lake. So I'm out of a job, too█ He looked on the edge of tears.

"Are you really a reverend mother?" Zelda asked su█ denly, knowing she had to take the chance.

"Well, of course I am," Hot Lips said, gesturing em█ phatically with her right hand, which held the marti█ glass, while she pulled up her bikini top with the othe█ "Can't you just tell by looking?"

"I need to talk to someone," Zelda said. "Will you he█ me?"

"Of course I will, darling," Hot Lips said. "Come wi█ me into the cabin, and we'll have a little talk and a litt█ martini, and get that mascara off your teeth all at onc█ Little smashed when you fixed your face, were yo█ Booze never helps, darling. Mother Emeritus kno█ that very well."

Boris waited until the girls were inside the cabi█ Then he turned to Steven Harris.

"I think the time has come for us to fish or cut bait█ he said. "Are you really serious about wanting to be █ doctor?"

"Of course I am."

"You want it bad enough to swallow your pride ar█ take the money to pay for it?"

"Charity, you mean?" Steve asked.

"Call it what you want to," Boris said. "Call it an investment in the future of mankind, in the health of the world."

"You really are an opera singer, aren't you?" Steve asked. "Zelda recognized you."

"I am not *an* opera singer, my dear boy," Boris said. "I am Boris Alexandrovich Korsky-Rimsakov, *the* world's greatest opera singer."

"And you're offering to give me the money to pay for my medical education?"

"*Me?* Don't be absurd. We'll get the Frogs to pay for it," Boris said. "You told me one time that you could talk to anyone in the world on that police radio. Is that so? Or had I been tippling?"

"I said you can be patched through to any police station in the world," Steve said.

"Come with me, my lovesick pal," Boris said. "I have a sudden urge to speak to Paris, France, the city of lovers." He walked to the radio, picked up the microphone, and asked, "What button do I push?"

"It doesn't work that way," Steve said, sitting down at the table. "Who do you want to talk to?"

"The desk sergeant at the Place de l'Opéra Station of the Paris gendarmerie," Boris said. "Can you call collect?"

"It's not a telephone," Steve said. He picked up the microphone. "This is Maine Zebra station," he said. "Patch me through to Montreal."

In about sixty seconds, he handed the microphone to Boris.

"Push the button to talk," he said, "and say 'over' when you've finished a sentence."

"Am I speaking with the Paris gendarmerie at the Place de l'Opéra station?" he asked. "Over."

"Yes. What sort of international crime can the Gendarmerie Nationale solve for you? Over."

"This is Boris Alexandrovich Korsky-Rimsakov," Boris said. "I have an announcement to make. My triumphant return to the Paris Opéra will be a medical benefit performance *magnifique*." He handed the microphone to Steve. "You may hang up. We now have to call New Orleans."

"Why New Orleans?" Steve said. "This is Maine Zebra, Paris, thank you, break it down, and Maine Zebra out."

"Fascinating!" Boris said. "What won't they think of next?"

"Why do we have to talk to New Orleans?" Steve asked, again.

"Hot Lips!" Boris shouted. "Knock it off in there. Steve's going to call New Orleans for us."

Hot Lips and Zelda came back in the room. Gone was the Salvation Army dress; gone was the mascara on her cheeks; gone was the mascara on her teeth. Gone, too, was the tightly brushed back hair; it now cascaded in golden strands down her shoulders.

"Notice anything different?" Zelda asked, shyly.

"What happened to that dress you were wearing?" Steve asked. "Aren't you afraid you'll catch cold dressed in shorts and a halter like that?"

"I'll take my chances," Zelda said.

"God, he's just like you are!" Hot Lips said to Boris. "He is simply unable to appreciate a beautiful woman."

Boris shut her off with an imperious palm: "You want to talk to Reverend Doctor Mother Bernadette of Lourdes at the Gates of Heaven Medical Center, right?"

"Please," Hot Lips said. "She's the chief of staff, so you'll have to use my name to get right through to her."

In just a matter of seconds, the New Orleans police radio operator, ever willing to come to the aid of distinguished theological and medical personnel, had the connection completed between Reverend Mother Emeritus Margaret H. W. Wilson, R.N., in Maine and Reverend Mother Bernadette of Lourdes, M.D., F.A.C.S., Chief of Staff of Gates of Heaven Medical Center.

"I'm ready for you, Reverend Mother," Steve said, handing her the microphone.

"Bernie? This is Maggie. I need a little favor. You're just going to have to push in one more chair in the medical school, dear, as a favor to me. And to Boris. And to Hawkeye and Trapper John. Over."

There was a pause.

"Did you get all that, Bernie?" Hot Lips said again. "Over."

"I've already talked to Trapper John and Hawkeye," Reverend Mother Doctor said. "I told them I'd let this guy into the medical school . . . finest kind, they said he was . . . but I told them no dice on finding some female for him. I want you to understand that, too, Maggie. Over."

"Oh," Hot Lips said, "you won't have to worry about *that,* Bernie! He's bringing his *own biologist* with him. Now, is there anything I can bring you from Maine? Over."

"Nothing, thank you. Good-bye, Reverend Mother. Over and out."

"Bye-bye, Reverend Mother Doctor," Hot Lips said. "Over and out."

The radio immediately snapped to life. "Zebra station, if you're finished fooling around, the father of the kidnapee wants to make another appeal for the return of his daughter. The ransom he's offering is now up to two million."

"Boy, can you imagine that kind of money?" Harris said.

Zelda picked up the microphone.

"Hello, Daddy?" she said. "Cool it. Everything's just fine."

Trooper Steven J. Harris, in full uniform, fainted. Learning that his little Zelda, whom he had loved from the first moment he looked into her eyes, was loaded *was quite a shock to him.* He still looked stunned eight hours later when, with the blessing of His Bureaucratic Majesty the governor (as he was described by Dr. Pierce), who waved the normal waiting period, he was united in holy matrimony with the lady, three minutes and six seconds, by Bulova watch, before the bride's mother arrived, blood in her eye, from New York with

the intention of stopping the ceremony, which she terme
then and later to be the greatest loss to the theater sinc
she herself had turned in her ballet slippers.

Despite the absence of the bride's mother, the wed
ing ceremony was a great success. A certain touch c
class was added by the presence not only of Sheik
Abdullah ben Abzug but also of his Islamic Majesty'
Ambassador Extraordinary and Plenipotentiary Sheik
El Noil Sniol, who together with the secretary of state
sang "I Love You Truly" during the recessional.

The ceremony, of course, was conducted by the Right
Reverend Mother Emeritus Margaret H. W. Wilson of
the God Is Love in All Forms Christian Church, Inc.
The bride was given in marriage by her father, who borrowed a suit for the occasion and was heard to remark
during the reception (the bartenders were Drs. Benjamin
Franklin Pierce and John Francis Xavier McIntyre) that
despite the English-sounding name, he was convinced his
new son-in-law must be a Greek, for who but a Greek
could meet, woo, and wed his little duckie-wuckie in
something under twelve hours?

Bonita Granville Spinopolous, however, truth to tell,
although she danced at the wedding, didn't make her
peace with her son-in-law until about a year later, when
Zelda presented her with a grandson. At that point,
Grandmother Spinopolous announced that anyone able to
father such an obvious future Barrymore couldn't be all
bad.